# Giants of America

★ ★ ★ ★

# The Founding Fathers

*James Madison*

★　　★　　★　　★　　★　　★

# JAMES MADISON

*The Home of James Madison*

## SYDNEY HOWARD GAY

ARLINGTON HOUSE　*New Rochelle, N.Y.*

*Library of Congress Catalog Card Number 78-111223*

SBN 87000–084–5

MANUFACTURED IN THE UNITED STATES OF AMERICA

# CONTENTS

# ILLUSTRATIONS

# JAMES MADISON

## CHAPTER I

### THE VIRGINIA MADISONS

JAMES MADISON was born on March 16, 1751, at Port Conway, Virginia; he died at Montpellier, in that State, on June 28, 1836. Mr. John Quincy Adams, recalling, perhaps, the death of his own father and of Jefferson on the same Fourth of July, and that of Monroe on a subsequent anniversary of that day, may possibly have seen a generous propriety in finding some equally appropriate commemoration for the death of another Virginian President. For it was quite possible that Virginia might think him capable of an attempt to conceal, what to her mind would seem to be an obvious intention of Providence: that all the children of the " Mother of Presidents " should be no less distinguished in their deaths than in their lives — that the " other dynasty," which John Randolph was wont to talk about, should no longer pretend to an equality with them, not merely in this world, but in the manner of going out of it. At any rate, he notes the date of Madison's death, the twenty-eighth day of June, as "the anniversary of the day on which the ratification of the Convention of Virginia in 1788 had affixed the seal of James Madison as the father of the Constitution of the United States, when his earthly part sank without a struggle into the grave, and a spirit, bright as the seraphim that surround the throne of Omnipotence, ascended to the bosom of his God." There can be no doubt of the deep sincerity of this tribute, whatever question there may be of its grammatical construction and its rhetoric, and although the date is erroneous. The ratification of the Constitution of the United States by the Virginia Convention was on June 25, not on June 28. It is the misfortune of our time that we have no living great men held in such universal veneration that their dying on common days like common mortals seems quite impossible. Half a century ago, however, the propriety of such providential arrangements appears to have been recognized almost as one of the "institutions." It was the newspaper gossip of that time that a "distinguished physician" declared that he would have kept a fourth ex-President alive to die on a Fourth of July, had the illustrious sick man been under his treatment. The patient himself, had he been consulted, might, in that case, possibly have declined to have a fatal illness prolonged a week to gratify the public fondness for patriotic coincidence. But Mr. Adams's appropriation of another anniversary answered all the purpose, for that he made a mistake as to the date does not seem to have been discovered.

It was accidental that Port Conway was the birthplace of Madison. His maternal grandfather, whose name was Conway, had a plantation at that place, and young Mrs. Madison happened to be there on a visit to her mother when her first child, James, was born. In the stately — not to say stilted — biography of him by William C. Rives, the christened name .of this lady is given as Eleanor. Mr. Rives may have thought it not in accordance with ancestral dignity that the mother of so distinguished a son should have been burdened with so commonplace and homely a name as Nelly. But we are afraid it is true that Nelly was her name. No other biographer than Mr. Rives, that we know of, calls her Eleanor. Even Madison himself permits "Nelly" to pass under his eyes and from his hands as his mother's name.

In 1833–34 there was some correspondence between him and Lyman C. Draper, the historian, which includes some notes upon the Madison genealogy. These, the ex-President writes, were "made out by a member of the family," and they may be considered, therefore, as having his sanction. The first record is, that "James Madison was the son of James Madison and Nelly Conway." On such authority Nelly, and not Eleanor, must be accepted as the mother's name. This, of course, is to be regretted from the Rives point of view; but perhaps the name had a less

familiar sound a century and a half ago; and no
doubt it was chosen by her parents without a
thought that their daughter might go into history
as the mother of a President, or that any higher
fortune could befall her than to be the respectable
head of a tobacco planter's family on the banks of
the Rappahannock.

This genealogical record further says that "his
[Madison's] ancestors, on both sides, were not
among the most wealthy of the country, but in
independent and comfortable circumstances." If
this comment was added at the ex-President's own
dictation, it was quite in accordance with his un-
pretentious character.[1]   One might venture to say

---

[1] Dr. Draper has kindly put into our hands the correspondence
between himself and Mr. Madison, and we copy these genealogical
notes in full, with the letter in which they were sent, as all that
the ex-President had to say about his ancestry : —

MONTPELLIER, *February* 1, 1834.
DEAR SIR, — I have received your letter of December 31st, and
inclose a sketch on the subject of it, made out by a member of the
family.            With friendly respects,
JAMES MADISON.

" James Madison was the son of James Madison and Nelly Conway.   He was born on the 5th of March, 1751 (O. S.), at Port
Conway, on the Rappahannock River, where she was at the time
on a visit to her mother residing there.

" His father was the son of Ambrose Madison and Frances
Taylor.   His mother was the daughter of Francis Conway and
Rebecca Catlett.

" His paternal grandfather was the son of John Madison and
Isabella Minor Todd.   His paternal grandmother, the daughter
of James Taylor and Martha Thompson.

" His maternal grandfather was the son of Edwin Conway and

as much of a Northern or a Western farmer. But
they did not farm in Virginia; they planted.
Mr. Rives says that the elder James was "a large
landed proprietor;" and he adds, "a large landed
estate in Virginia . . . was a mimic commonwealth, with its foreign and domestic relations,
and its regular administrative hierarchy." The
"foreign relations" were the shipping, once a
year, a few hogsheads of tobacco to a London
factor; the "mimic commonwealths" were clusters
of negro huts; and the "administrative hierarchy"
was the priest, who was more at home at the tavern
or a horse-race than in the discharge of his clerical
duties.

As Mr. Madison had only to say of his immediate ancestors — which seems to be all he knew
about them — that they were in "independent
and comfortable circumstances," so he was, apparently, as little inclined to talk about himself;
even at that age when it is supposed that men who
have enjoyed celebrity find their own lives the
most agreeable of subjects. In answer to Dr.
Draper's inquiries he wrote this modest letter,
now for the first time published : —

Elizabeth Thornton. His maternal grandmother, the daughter of
John Catlett and —— Gaines.

"His father was a planter, and dwelt on the estate now called
Montpellier, where he died February 27, 1801, in the 78th year of
his age. His mother died at the same place in 1829, February
11th, in the 98th year of her age.

"His grandfathers were also planters. It appears that his ancestors, on both sides, were not among the most wealthy of the
country, but in independent and comfortable circumstances."

MONTPELLIER, *August* 9, 1833.

DEAR SIR, — Since your letter of the 3d of June
came to hand, my increasing age and continued mala-
dies, with the many attentions due from me, had caused
a delay in acknowledging it, for which these circumstances must be an apology, in your case, as I have been
obliged to make them in others.

You wish me to refer you to sources of printed information on my career in life, and it would afford me
pleasure to do so ; but my recollection on the subject is
very defective. It occurs [to me] that there was a bio-
graphical volume in an enlarged edition compiled by
General or Judge Rodgers of Pennsylvania, and which
may perhaps have included my name, among others.
When or where it was published I cannot say. To this
reference I can only add generally the newspapers at
the seat of government and elsewhere during the elec-
tioneering periods, when I was one of the objects under
review. I need scarcely remark that a life, which has
been so much a public life, must of course be traced in
the public transactions in which it was involved, and
that the most important of them are to be found in
documents already in print, or soon to be so.

With friendly respects,     JAMES MADISON.

LYMAN C. DRAPER, Lockport, N. Y.

The genealogical statement, it will be observed,
does not go farther back than Mr. Madison's great-
grandfather, John. Mr. Rives supposes that this
John was the son of another John who, as " the
pious researches of kindred have ascertained,"
took out a patent for land about 1653 between the
North and York rivers on the shores of Chesa-

peake Bay. The same writer further assumes that
this John was descended from Captain Isaac Madison, whose name appears " in a document in the
State Paper Office at London containing a list of
the Colonists in 1623." From Sainsbury's Calendar [1] we learn something more of this Captain Isaac
than this mere mention. Under date of January
24, 1623, there is this record: "Captain Powell,
gunner, of James City, is dead; Capt. Nuce (?),
Capt. Maddison, Lieut. Craddock's brother, and
divers more of the chief men reported dead." But
either the report was not altogether true or there
was another Isaac Maddison, for the name appears among the signatures to a letter dated about a
month later — February 20 — from the governor,
council, and Assembly of Virginia to the king. It
is of record, also, that four months later still, on
June 4, " Capt. Isaac and Mary Maddison " were
before the governor and council as witnesses in
the case of Greville Pooley and Cicely Jordan,
between whom there was a " supposed contract of
marriage," made " three or four days after her
husband's death." But the lively widow, it seems,
afterward " contracted herself to Will Ferrar before the governor and council, and disavowed the
former contract," and the case therefore became so
complicated that the court was " not able to decide

---

[1] *Calendar of State Papers*, Colonial Series, 1574–1660, Preserved in the State Paper Department of Her Majesty's Public
Record Office, edited by W. Noel Sainsbury, Esq., etc. London,
1860.

so nice a difference." What Captain Isaac and Mary Maddison knew about the matter the record does not tell us; but the evidence is conclusive that if there was but one Isaac Maddison in Virginia in 1623 he did not die in January of that year. Probably there was but one, and he, as Rives assumes, was the Captain Madyson of whose "achievement," as Rives calls it, there is a brief narrative in John Smith's "General History of Virginia."

Besides the record in Sainsbury's Calendar of the rumor of the death of this Isaac in Virginia, in January, 1623, his signature to a letter to the king in February, and his appearance as a witness before the council in the case of the widow Jordan, in June, it appears by Hotten's Lists of colonists, taken from the Records in the English State Paper Department, that Captain Isacke Maddeson and Mary Maddeson were living in 1624 at West and Sherlow Hundred Island. The next year, at the same place, he is on the list of dead; and there is given under the same date "The muster of Mrs. Mary Maddison, widow, aged 30 years." Her family consisted of "Katherin Layden, child, aged 7 years," and two servants. Katherine, it may be assumed, was the daughter of the widow Mary and Captain Isaac, and their only child. These "musters," it should be said, appear always to have been made with great care, and there is therefore hardly a possibility that a son, if there were one, was omitted in the numeration of the widow's family, while the name and age of the little girl, and the names and ages of the two servants, the date of their arrival in Virginia, and the name of the ship that each came in, are all carefully given. The conclusion is inevitable: Isaac Maddison left no male descendants, and President Madison's earliest ancestor in Virginia, if it was not his great-grandfather John, must be looked for somewhere else.

Mr. Rives knew nothing of these Records. His first volume was published before either Sainsbury's Calendar or Hotten's Lists; and the researches on which he relied, " conducted by a distinguished member of the Historical Society of Virginia " in the English State Paper Office, were, so far as they related to the Madisons, incomplete and worthless. The family was not, apparently, " coeval with the foundation of the Colony," and did not arrive " among the earliest of the emigrants in the New World." That distinction cannot be claimed for James Madison, nor is there any reason for supposing that he believed it could be. He seemed quite content with the knowledge that so far back as his great-grandfather his ancestors had been respectable people, " in independent and comfortable circumstances."

Of his own generation there were seven children, of whom James was the eldest, and alone became of any note, except that the rest were reputable and contented people in their stations of life. A hundred years ago the Arcadian Virginia, for which

Governor Berkeley had thanked God so devoutly,
— when there was not a free school nor a press in
the province, — had passed away.   The elder Madison resolved, so Mr. Rives tells us, that his children
should have advantages of education which had not
been within his own reach, and that they should all
enjoy them equally.   James was sent to a school
where he could at least begin the studies which
should fit him to enter college.   Of the master
of that school we know nothing except that he
was a Scotchman, of the name of Donald Robertson, and that many years afterward, when his son
was an applicant for office to Madison, then secretary of state, the pupil gratefully remembered
his old master, and indorsed upon the application
that "the writer is son of Donald Robertson, the
learned Teacher in King and Queen County, Virginia."

The preparatory studies for college were finished
at home under the clergyman of the parish, the
Rev. Thomas Martin, who was a member of Mr.
Madison's family, perhaps as a private tutor, perhaps as a boarder.   It is quite likely that it was
by the advice of this gentleman — who was from
New Jersey — that the lad was sent to Princeton
instead of to William and Mary College in Virginia.   At Princeton, at any rate, he entered at
the age of eighteen, in 1769 ; or, to borrow Mr.
Rives's eloquent statement of the fact, " the young
Virginian, invested with the *toga virilis* of anticipated manhood, we now see launched on that

disciplinary career which is to form him for the future struggles of life."

One of his biographers says that he shortened his collegiate term by taking in one year the studies of the junior and senior years, but that he remained another twelve-month at Princeton for the sake of acquiring Hebrew. On his return home he undertook the instruction of his younger brothers and sisters, while pursuing his own studies. Still another biographer asserts that he began immediately to read law, but Rives gives some evidence that he devoted himself to theology. This and his giving himself to Hebrew for a year point to the ministry as his chosen profession. But if we rightly interpret his own words, he had little strength or spirit for a pursuit of any sort. His first "struggle of life" was apparently with ill-health, and the career he looked forward to was a speedy journey to another world. In a letter to a friend (November, 1772) he writes: "I am too dull and infirm now to look out for extraordinary things in this world, for I think my sensations for many months have intimated to me not to expect a long or healthy life; though it may be better with me after some time; but I hardly dare expect it, and therefore have little spirit or elasticity to set about anything that is difficult in acquiring, and useless in possessing after one has exchanged time for eternity." In the same letter he assures his friend that he approves of his choice of history and morals as the subjects of his winter studies;

but, he adds, "I doubt not but you design to season them with a little divinity now and then, which, like the philosopher's stone in the hands of a good man, will turn them and every lawful acquirement into the nature of itself, and make them more precious than fine gold."

The bent of his mind at this time seems to have been decidedly religious. He was a diligent student of the Bible, and, Mr. Rives says, "he explored the whole history and evidences of Christianity on every side, through clouds of witnesses and champions for and against, from the fathers and schoolmen down to the infidel philosophers of the eighteenth century." So wide a range of theological study is remarkable in a youth of only two or three and twenty years of age ; but, remembering that he was at this time living at home, it is even more remarkable that in the house of an ordinary planter in Virginia a hundred and twenty years ago could be found a library so rich in theology as to admit of study so exhaustive. But in Virginia history nothing is impossible.

His studies on this subject, however, whether wide or limited, bore good fruit. Religious intolerance was at that time common in his immediate neighborhood, and it aroused him to earnest and open opposition ; nor did that opposition cease till years afterward, when freedom of conscience was established by law in Virginia, largely by his labors and influence. Even in 1774, when all the colonies were girding themselves for the coming

revolutionary conflict, he turned aside from a discussion of the momentous question of the hour, in
a letter to his friend [1] in Philadelphia, and exclaimed with unwonted heat : —

" But away with politics ! . . . That diabolical, hell-
conceived principle of persecution rages among some ;
and, to their eternal infamy, the clergy can furnish
their quota of imps for such purposes.  There are at
this time in the adjacent country not less than five or
six well-meaning men in close jail for publishing their
religious sentiments, which in the main are very ortho-
dox.  I have neither patience to hear, talk, or think of
anything relative to this matter ; for I have squabbled
and scolded, abused and ridiculed so long about it to little purpose that I am without common patience."

These are stronger terms than the mild-tem-
pered Madison often indulged in.  But he felt
strongly.  Probably he, no more than many other
wiser and older men, understood what was to be
the end of the political struggle which was getting
so earnest ; but evidently in his mind it was religious rather than civil liberty which was to be
guarded.  "If the Church of England," he says
in the same letter, " had been the established and
general religion in all the Northern colonies, as it
has been among us here, and uninterrupted harmony had prevailed throughout the continent, it is

[1] The letters to a friend, from which we have quoted, were
written to William Bradford, Jr., of Philadelphia, afterward attorney-general in Washington's administration.  They are given
in full in *The Writings of James Madison,* vol. i.

clear to me that slavery and subjection might and would have been gradually insinuated among us."

He congratulated his friend that they had not permitted the tea-ships to break cargo in Philadelphia; and Boston, he hoped, would " conduct matters with as much discretion as they seem to do with boldness." These things were interesting and important; but " away with politics! Let me address you as a student and philosopher, and not as a patriot." Shut off from any contact with the stirring incidents of that year in the towns of the coast, he lost something of the sense of proportion. To a young student, solitary, ill in body, perhaps a trifle morbid in mind, a little discontented that all the learning gained at Princeton could find no better use than to save schooling for the six youngsters at home, — to him it may have seemed that liberty was more seriously threatened by that outrage, under his own eyes, of " five or six well-meaning men in close jail for publishing their religious sentiments," than by any tax which Parliament could contrive. Not that he overestimated the importance of this wrong, but that he underestimated the importance of that. He was not long, however, in getting the true perspective.

# CHAPTER II

## THE YOUNG STATESMAN

MADISON's place, both from temperament and from want of physical vigor, was in the council, not in the field. One of his early biographers says that he joined a military company, raised in his own county, in preparation for war ; but this, there can hardly be a doubt, is an error. He speaks with enthusiasm of the "high-spirited" volunteers, who came forward to defend "the honor and safety of their country ; " but there is no intimation that he chose for himself that way of showing his patriotism. But of the Committee of Safety, appointed in his county in 1774, he was made a member, — perhaps the youngest, for he was then only twenty-three years old.

Eighteen months afterward he was elected a delegate to the Virginia Convention of 1776, and this he calls "my first entrance into public life." It gave him also an opportunity for some distinction, which, whatever may have been his earlier plans, opened public life to him as a career. The first work of the convention was to consider and adopt a series of resolutions instructing the Virginian delegates in the Continental Congress, then in session at Philadelphia, to urge an immediate declaration of independence. The next matter was to frame a Bill of Rights and a Constitution of government for the province. Madison was made a member of the committee to which this latter subject was referred. One question necessarily came up for consideration which had for him a peculiar interest, and in any discussion of which he, no doubt, felt quite at ease. This was concerning religious freedom. An article in the proposed Declaration of Rights provided that "all men should enjoy the fullest toleration in the exercise of religion, according to the dictates of conscience, unpunished and unrestrained by the magistrate, unless, under color of religion, any man disturb the peace, happiness, or safety of society." It does not appear that Mr. Madison offered any objection to the article in the committee; but when the report was made to the convention he moved an amendment. He pointed out the distinction between the recognition of an absolute right and the toleration of its exercise; for toleration implies the power of jurisdiction. He proposed, therefore, instead of providing that "all men should enjoy the fullest toleration in the exercise of religion," to declare that "all men are equally entitled to the full and free exercise of it according to the dictates of conscience;" and that "no man or class of men ought, on account of religion, to be invested with peculiar emoluments or privileges, nor subjected to any penalties or disabilities, unless, under color of religion, the preservation of equal liberty and the existence of the state be manifestly endangered." This distinction between the assertion of a right and the promise to grant a privilege only needed to be pointed out. But Mr. Madison evidently meant more; he meant not only that religious freedom should be assured, but that an Established Church, which, as we have already seen, he believed to be dangerous to liberty, should be prohibited. Possibly the convention was not quite ready for this latter step; or possibly its members thought that, as the greater includes the less, should freedom of conscience be established a state church would be impossible, and the article might therefore be stripped of supererogation and verbiage. At any rate, it was reduced one half, and finally adopted in this simpler form: " That religion, or the duty we owe to our Creator, and the manner of discharging it, can be directed only by reason and conviction, not by force or violence; and, therefore, all men are equally entitled to the free exercise of religion according to the dictates of conscience." Thus it stands to this day in the Bill of Rights of Virginia, and of other States which subsequently made it their own, possessing for us the personal interest of being the first public work of the coming statesman.

Madison was thenceforth for the next forty years a public man. Of the first Assembly under the new Constitution he was elected a member. For the next session also he was a candidate, but failed to be returned for a reason as creditable to him as it was uncommon then, whatever it may be now, in Virginia. "The sentiments and manners of the parent nation," Mr. Rives says, still prevailed in Virginia, "and the modes of canvassing for popular votes in that country were generally practiced. The people not only tolerated, but expected and even required, to be courted and treated. No candidate who neglected those attentions could be elected." But the times, Mr. Madison thought, seemed "to favor a more chaste mode of conducting elections," and he "determined to attempt, by an example, to introduce it." He failed signally; "the sentiments and manners of the parent nation" were too much for him. He solicited no votes; nobody got drunk at his expense; and he lost the election. An attempt was made to contest the return of his opponent on the ground of corrupt influence, but, adds Mr. Rives, in his sesquipedalian measure, "for the want of adequate proof to sustain the allegations of the petition which in such cases it is extremely difficult to obtain with the requisite precision, the proceeding was unavailing except as a perpetual protest, upon the legislative records of the country, against a dangerous abuse, of which one of her sons, so qualified to serve her, and destined to be one of her chief ornaments, was the early though temporary victim." Mr. Rives does not mean that Mr. Madison was for a little while in early life the victim of a vicious habit, but that he lost votes because he would do nothing to encourage it in others.

The country lost a good representative, but their loss was his gain. The Assembly immediately elected him a member of the governor's council, and in this position he so grew in public favor that, two years afterward (1780), he was chosen as a delegate to the Continental Congress. He was still under thirty, and had he been even a more brilliant young man than he really was, it would not have been to his discredit had he only been seen for the next year or two, if seen at all, in the background. He had taken his seat among men, every one of whom, probably, was his senior, and among whom were many of the wisest men in the country, not " older " merely, but " better soldiers."

If not the darkest, at least there was no darker year in the Revolution than that of 1780. Within a few days of his arrival at Philadelphia, Madison wrote to Jefferson — then governor of Virginia — his opinion of the state of the country. It was gloomy but not exaggerated. The only bright spot he could see was the chance that Clinton's expedition to South Carolina might be a failure; but within little more than a month from the date of his letter, Lincoln was compelled to surrender Charleston, and the whole country south of Virginia seemed about to fall into the hands of the enemy. Could he have foreseen that calamity, his apprehensions might have been changed to despair; for he writes : —

" Our army threatened with an immediate alternative
of disbanding or living on free quarter ; the public treasury empty ; public credit exhausted, nay, the private
credit of purchasing agents employed, I am told, as far
as it will bear ; Congress complaining of the extortion of
the people, the people of the improvidence of Congress,
and the army of both ; our affairs requiring the most
mature and systematic measures, and the urgency of
occasions admitting only of temporary expedients, and
these expedients generating new difficulties ; Congress
recommending plans to the several States for execution,
and the States separately rejudging the expediency of
such plans, whereby the same distrust of concurrent
exertions that had damped the ardor of patriotic individuals must produce the same effect among the States
themselves ; an old system of finance discarded as incom-
petent to our necessities, an untried and precarious one
substituted, and a total stagnation in prospect between
the end of the former and the operation of the latter.
These are the outlines of the picture of our public situation. I leave it to your own imagination to fill them up."

He saw more clearly, perhaps, after the experience of one session of Congress, the true cause of
all these troubles; at any rate, he was able, in a
letter written in November of that year (1780), to
state it tersely and explicitly. The want of money,
he wrote to a friend, " is the source of all our public difficulties and misfortunes. One or two millions of guineas properly applied would diffuse
vigor and satisfaction throughout the whole military department, and would expel the enemy from
every part of the United States."

But nobody knew better than he the difficulty of raising funds except by borrowing abroad, and that this was a precarious reliance. There must be some sort of substitute for money. In specific taxation he had no faith. Such taxes, if paid at all, would be paid, virtually, in the paper currency or certificates of the States, and these had already fallen to the ratio of one hundred to one; they kept on falling till they reached the rate of a thousand to one, and then soon became altogether worthless. When the estimate for the coming year was under consideration, he proposed to Congress that the States should be advised to abandon the issue of this paper currency. " It met," he says, " with so cool a reception that I did not much urge it." The sufficient answer to the proposition was, that " the practice was manifestly repugnant to the Acts of Congress," and as these were disregarded and could not be enforced, a mere remonstrance would be quite useless. The Union was little more than a name under the feeble bonds of the Confederation, and each State was a law unto itself. Not that in this case there was much reasonable ground for complaint; for what else could the States do? Where there was no money there must be something to take its place; a promise to pay must be accepted instead of payment. The paper answered a temporary purpose, though it was plain that in the end it would be good for nothing.

The evil, however, was manifestly so great that

there was only the more reason for trying to mitigate it, if it could not be cured. Madison, like
the rest, had his remedy. He proposed, in a letter to one of his colleagues, that the demand for
army supplies should be duly apportioned among
the people, their collection rigorously enforced, and
payment made in interest-bearing certificates, not
transferable, but to be redeemed at a specified
time after the war was over. The plan would undoubtedly have put a stop to the circulation of
a vast volume of paper money if the producers
would have exchanged the products of their labor
for certificates, useless at the time of exchange,
and having only a possible prospective value in
case of the successful termination of an uncertain
war. Patriotic as the people were, they neither
would nor could have submitted to such a law, nor
had Congress the power to enforce it. But Mr.
Madison did not venture apparently to urge his
plan beyond its suggestion to his colleague.

Why the Assembly of Virginia should have proposed to elect an extra delegate to Congress, early
in 1781, is not clear, unless it be that one of the
number, Joseph Jones, being also a member of
the Assembly, passed much of his time in Richmond.
It does not appear, however, that the delegate
extraordinary was ever sent, perhaps because it
was known to Mr. Madison's friends that it would
be a mortification to him. There was certainly no
good reason for any distrust of either his ability
or his industry. One could hardly be otherwise

than industrious who had it in him — if the story
be true — to take but three hours out of the twenty-
four for sleep during the last year of his college
course, that he might crowd the studies of two
years into one. He seemed to love work for its
own sake, and he was a striking example of how
much virtue there is in steadiness of pursuit. Not
that he had at this time any special goal for his
ambition. His aim seemed to be simply to do the
best he could wherever he might be placed; to
discharge faithfully, and to the best of such ability
as he had, whatever duty was intrusted to him.
His report of the proceedings in the congressional
session of 1782–83, and the letters written during
those years and the year before, show that he was
not merely diligent but absorbed in the duties of
his office.

He was more faithful to his constituents than
his constituents sometimes were to him. Anything that might happen at that period for want
of money can hardly be a matter of surprise; but
Virginia, even then, should have been able, it
would seem, to find enough to enable its members
of Congress to pay their board-bills. He complains gently in his Addisonian way of the incon-
venience to which he was put for want of funds.
"I cannot," he writes to Edmund Randolph, "in
any way make you more sensible of the importance
of your kind attention to pecuniary remittances for
me, than by informing you that I have for some
time past been a pensioner on the favor of Hayne

Solomon, a Jew broker." A month later he writes, that to draw bills on Virginia has been tried, "but in vain;" nobody would buy them; and he adds, "I am relapsing fast into distress. The case of my brethren is equally alarming." Within a week he again writes: "I am almost ashamed to reiterate my wants so incessantly to you, but they begin to be so urgent that it is impossible to suppress them." But the Good Samaritan, Solomon, is still an unfailing reliance. "The kindness of our little friend in Front Street, near the coffee house, is a fund which will preserve me from extremities; but I never resort to it without great mortification, as he obstinately rejects all recompense. The price of money is so usurious that he thinks it ought to be extorted from none but those who aim at profitable speculations. To a necessitous delegate he gratuitously spares a supply out of his private stock." It is a pretty picture of the simplicity of the early days of the Republic. Between the average modern member and the money-broker, under such circumstances, there would lurk, probably, a contract for carrying the mails or for Indian supplies.

Relief, however, came at last. An appeal was made in a letter to the governor of Virginia, which was so far public that anybody about the executive office might read it. The answer to this letter, says Mr. Madison, "seems to chide our urgency." But there soon came a bill for two hundred dollars, which, he adds, "very seasonably enabled me to replace a loan by which I had anticipated it. About three hundred and fifty more (not less) would redeem me completely from the class of debtors." It is to be hoped it came without further chiding.[1]

The young member was not less attentive to his congressional duties because of these little difficulties in the personal ways and means. Military movements seem, without altogether escaping his attention, to have interested him the least. In his letters to the public men at home, which were meant in some degree to give such information as in later times the newspapers supplied, questions relating to army affairs, even news directly from the army, occupy the least space. They are not always, for that reason, altogether entertaining reading. One would be glad, occasionally, to exchange their sonorous and rounded periods for any expression of quick, impulsive feeling. "I return you," he writes to Pendleton, "my fervent congratulations on the glorious success of the combined armies at York and Gloucester. We have had from the Commander-in-Chief an official report of the fact," — and so forth and so forth; and then for a page or more is a discussion of the condition of British possessions in the East Indies, that "rich

[1] The members of Congress were paid, at that time, by the States they represented. Virginia allowed her delegates their family expenses, including three servants and four horses, house rent and fuel, two dollars a mile for travel, and twenty dollars a day when in attendance on Congress. The members were required to render an account quarterly of their household expenses, and the State paid them when she had any money.

source of their commerce and credit, severed from
them, perhaps forever;" of "the predatory conquest
of Eustatia;" and of the "relief of Gibraltar, which
was merely a negative advantage;" — all to show
that "it seems scarcely possible for them much
longer to shut their ears against the voice of
peace." There is not a word in all this that is not
quite true, pertinent, reflective, and becoming a
statesman; but neither is there a word of sympa-
thetic warmth and patriotic fervor which at that
moment made the heart of a whole people beat
quicker at the news of a great victory, and in the
hope that the cause was gained at last.

All the letters have this preternatural solemnity,
as if each was a study in style after the favorite
Addisonian model. One wonders if he did not, in
the privacy of his own room and with the door
locked, venture to throw his hat to the ceiling and
give one hurrah under his breath at the discom-
fiture of the vain and self-sufficient Cornwallis.
But he seems never to have been a young man.
At one and twenty he gravely warned his friend
Bradford not "to suffer those impertinent fops
that abound in every city to divert you from your
business and philosophical amusements. . . . You
will make them respect and admire you more by
showing your indignation at their follies, and by
keeping them at a becoming distance." It was his
loss, however, and our gain. He was one of the
men the times demanded, and without whom they
would have been quite different times and followed

by quite different results. The sombre hue of his life was due partly, no doubt, to natural temperament; partly to the want of health in his earlier manhood, which led him to believe that his days were numbered; but quite as much, if not more than either, to a keen sense of the responsibility resting upon those to whom had fallen the conduct of public affairs.

# CHAPTER III

MADISON had grown steadily in the estimation
of his colleagues, as is shown, especially in 1783,
by the frequency of his appointment upon important committees. He was a member of that one
to which was intrusted the question of national
finances, and it is plain, even in his own modest
report of the debates of that session, that he took
an important part in the long discussions of the
subject, and exercised a marked influence upon the
result. The position of the government was one
of extreme difficulty. To tide over an immediate
necessity, a further loan had been asked of France
in 1782, and bills were drawn against it without
waiting for acceptance. It was not very likely,
but it was not impossible, that the bills might go
to protest; but even should they be honored, so
irregular a proceeding was a humiliating acknowledgment of poverty and weakness, to which some
of the delegates, Mr. Madison among them, were
extremely sensitive.

The national debt altogether was not less than
forty million dollars. To provide for the interest on this debt, and a fund for expenses, it was

necessary to raise about three million dollars annu-
ally. But the sum actually contributed for the
support of the confederate government in 1782 was
only half a million dollars. This was not from
any absolute inability on the part of the people to
pay more; for the taxes before the war were more
than double that sum, and for the first three or
four years of the war it was computed that, with
the depreciation of paper money, the people submitted to an annual tax of about twenty million
dollars. The real difficulty lay in the character of
the Confederation. Congress might contrive but
it could not command. The States might agree, or
they might disagree, or any two or more of them
might only agree to disagree; and they were more
likely to do either of the last two than the first.
There was no power of coercion anywhere. All
that Congress could do was to try to frame laws
that would reconcile differences, and bring thirteen
supreme governments upon some common ground
of agreement. To distract and perplex it still
more, it stood face to face with a well-disciplined
and veteran army which might at any moment,
could it find a leader to its mind, march upon
Philadelphia and deal with Congress as Cromwell
dealt with the Long Parliament. There were some
men, probably, in that body, who would not have
been sorry to see that precedent followed. Washington might have done it if he would. Gates
probably would have done it if he could.

To avert this threatened danger; to contrive

taxation that should so far please the taxed that they would refrain from using the power in their hands to escape altogether any taxation for general purposes, — was the knotty problem this Congress had to solve in order to save the Confederacy from dissolution. There was no want of plans and expedients ; neither were there wanting men in that body who clearly understood the conditions of the problem, and how it might be solved, and whose aim was direct and unfaltering. Chief among them were Hamilton, Wilson, Ellsworth, and Madison. However wrong-headed, or weak, or intemperate others may have been, these men were usually found together on important questions ; differing sometimes in details, but unmoved by passion or prejudice, and strong from reserved force, they overwhelmed their opponents at the right moment with irresistible argument and by weight of character.

In the discussion of the more important questions Mr. Madison is conspicuous — conspicuous without being obtrusive. A reader of the debates can hardly fail to be struck with his familiarity with English constitutional law, and its application to the necessities of this offshoot of the English people in setting up a government for themselves. The stores of knowledge he drew upon must needs have been laid up in the years of quiet study at home before he entered upon public life. For there was no congressional library then where a member could " cram " for debate ; and — though

Philadelphia already had a fair public library —
the member who was armed at all points must
have equipped himself before entering Congress.
In this respect Madison probably had no equal,
except Hamilton, and possibly Ellsworth. To the
need of such a library, however, he and others
were not insensible. As chairman of a committee
he reported a list of books " proper for the use
of Congress," and advised their purchase. The
report declared that certain authorities upon international law, treaties, negotiations, and other questions of legislation were absolutely indispensable,
and that the want of them " was manifest in
several Acts of Congress." But the Congress was
not to be moved by a little thing of that sort.

The attitude of his own State sometimes embar-
rassed him in the satisfactory discharge of his duty
as a legislator. The earliest distinction he won
after entering Congress was as chairman of a
committee to enforce upon Mr. Jay, then minister
to Spain, the instructions to adhere tenaciously to
the right of navigation on the Mississippi in his
negotiations for an alliance with that power. Mr.
Madison, in his dispatch, maintained the American
side of the question with a force and clearness to
which no subsequent discussion of the subject ever
added anything. He left nothing unsaid that
could be said to sustain the right either on the
ground of expediency, of national comity, or of
international law; and his arguments were not
only in accordance with his own convictions, but

with the instructions of the Assembly of his own State. It was a question of deep interest to Virginia, whose western boundary at that time was the Mississippi. But Virginia soon afterward shifted her position. The course of the war in the Southern States in the winter of 1780–81 aroused in Georgia and the Carolinas renewed anxiety for an alliance with Spain. The fear of their people was that, in case of the necessity for a sudden peace while the British troops were in possession of those States or parts of them, they might be compelled to remain as British territory under the application of the rule of *uti possidetis*. It was urged, therefore, that the right to the Mississippi should be surrendered to Spain, if it were made the condition of an alliance. In deference to her neighbors, Virginia proposed that Mr. Jay should be reinstructed accordingly.

Mr. Madison was not in the least shaken in his conviction. With him, the question was one of right rather than of expediency. But not many at that time ventured to doubt that representatives must implicitly obey the instructions of their constituents. He yielded; but not till he had appealed to the Assembly to reconsider their decision. The scale was turned; in deference to the wishes of the Southern States new orders were sent to Mr. Jay. Mr. Madison, however, had not long to wait for his justification. When the immediate danger, which had so alarmed the South, had passed away, Virginia returned to her original

position.  New instructions were again sent to her
representatives, and Mr. Jay was once more advised by Congress that on the Mississippi question his government would yield nothing.

On another question, two years afterward, Mr.
Madison refused to accept a position of inconsistency in obedience to instructions which his State
attempted to force upon him.  No one saw more
clearly than he how absolutely necessary to the
preservation of the Confederacy was the settlement of its financial affairs on some sound and
just basis ; and no one labored more earnestly and
more intelligently than he to bring about such a
settlement.  Congress had proposed in 1781 a tax
upon imports, each State to appoint its own col-
lectors, but the revenue to be paid over to the
federal government to meet the expenses of the
war.  Rhode Island alone, at first, refused her
assent to this scheme.  An impost law of five per
cent. upon certain imports and a specific duty
upon others for twenty-five years were an essential
part of the plan of 1783 to provide a revenue to
meet the interest on the public debt and for other
general purposes.  That Rhode Island would continue obstinate on this point was more than probable ; and the only hope of moving her was that
she should be shamed or persuaded into compliance by the combined influence of all the other
States.

Mr. Madison was as bitter as he could ever be
in his reflections upon that State, whose course,

he thought, showed a want of any sense of honor
or of patriotism.  Virginia, he argued, should re-
buke her by making her own compliance with the
law the more emphatic, as an example for all the
rest.  But Virginia did exactly the other thing.
At the moment when debate upon the revenue
law was the most earnest, and the prospect of carrying it the most hopeful; when a committee appointed by Congress had already started on their
journey northward to expostulate with, and if possible conciliate, Rhode Island, — at that critical
moment came news from Virginia that she had
revoked her assent of a previous session to the impost law.  This was equivalent to instructing her
delegates in Congress to oppose any such measure.
The situation was an awkward one for a representative who had put himself among the foremost of
those who were pushing this policy, and who had
been making invidious reflections upon a State
which opposed it.  The rule that the will of the
constituents should govern the representative, he
now declared, had its exceptions, and here was a
case in point.  He continued to enforce the necessity of a general law to provide a revenue, though
his arguments were no longer pointed with the
selfishness and want of patriotism shown by the
people of Rhode Island.  In the end his firmness
was justified by Virginia, who again shifted her
position when the new act was submitted to her.

The operation of the law was limited to five and
twenty years.  This Hamilton opposed and Madi-

son supported ; and in this difference some of
the biographers of both see the foreshadowing of
future parties. But it is more likely that neither
of those statesmen thought of their difference of
opinion as difference of principle. The question
was, whether anything could be gained by a deference to that party which, both felt at that time,
threatened to throw away, in adhering to the state-
rights doctrine, all that was gained by the Revolution. They were agreed upon the necessity of a
general law, supreme in all the States, to meet
the obligation of a debt contracted for the general
good. Unless — wrote Madison in February —
" unless some amicable and adequate arrangements
be speedily taken for adjusting all the subsisting
accounts and discharging the public engagements,
a dissolution of the Union will be inevitable." He
was willing, therefore, to temporize, that the necessary assent of the State to such a law might be
gained. Nobody hoped that the public debt would
be paid off in twenty-five years ; but to assume to
levy a federal tax in the States for a longer period,
or till the debt should be discharged, might so
arouse state jealousy that it would be impossible
to get an assent to the law anywhere. If the
law for twenty-five years should be accepted, the
threatened destruction of the government would be
escaped for the present, and it might, at the end
of a quarter of a century, be easy to reënact the
law. At any rate, the evil day would be put off.
This was Madison's reasoning.

But Hamilton did not believe in putting off a
crisis.   He had no faith in the permanency of the
government as then organized.   If he were right,
what was the use or the wisdom of postponing a
catastrophe till to-morrow?   A possible escape
from it might be even more difficult to-morrow
than to-day.   The essential difference between
the two men was, that Madison only feared what
Hamilton positively knew, or thought he knew.
It was a difference of faith.   Madison hoped something would turn up in the course of twenty-five
years.   Hamilton did not believe that anything
good could turn up under the feeble rule of the
Confederation.   He would have presented to the
States, then and there, the question, Would they
surrender to the confederate government the right
of taxation so long as that government thought it
necessary?   If not, then the Confederation was a
rope of sand, and the States had resolved themselves into thirteen separate and independent governments.   Therefore he opposed the condition of
twenty-five years, and voted against the bill.

Nevertheless, when it became the law he gave it
his heartiest support, and was appointed one of a
committee of three to prepare an address, which
Madison wrote, to commend it to the acceptance
of the States.   Indeed, the last serious effort made
on behalf of the measure was made by Hamilton,
who used all his eloquence and influence to induce the legislature of his own State to ratify it.
It was the law against his better judgment; but

being the law, he did his best to secure its recognition. But it failed of hearty support in most of the States, while in New York and Pennsylvania compliance with it was absolutely refused. Nothing, therefore, would have been lost had Hamilton's firmness prevailed in Congress; and nothing was gained by Madison's deference to the doctrine of state rights, unless it was that the question of a " more perfect Union " was put off to a more propitious time, when a reconstruction of the government under a new federal Constitution was possible. Meanwhile Congress borrowed the money to pay the interest on money already borrowed; the confederate government floundered deeper and deeper into inextricable difficulties; the thirteen ships of state drifted farther and farther apart, with a fair promise of a general wreck.

But the bill contained another compromise which was not temporary, and once made could not be easily unmade. Agreed to now, it became a condition of the adoption of the federal Constitution four years later; and there, as nobody now is so blind as not to see, it was the source of infinite mischief for nearly a century, till a third reconstruction of the Union was brought about by the war of 1861–65. The Articles of Confederation required that " all charges of war and all other expenses that shall be incurred for the common defense or general welfare " should be borne by the States in proportion to the value of their lands. It was proposed to amend this provision

of the Constitution, and for lands substitute population, exclusive of Indians not taxed, as the basis
for taxation. But here arose at once a new and
perplexing question. There were, chiefly in one
portion of the country, about 750,000 " persons
held to service or labor," — the euphuism for negro slaves which, evolved from some tender and
sentimental conscience, came into use at this period. Should these, recognized only as property
by state law, be counted as 750,000 persons by
the laws of the United States? [1] Or should they,
in the enumeration of population, be reckoned, in
accordance with the civil law, as *pro nullis, pro
mortuis, pro quadrupedibus,* and therefore not to
be counted at all? Or should they, as those who
owned them insisted, be counted, if included in the
basis of taxation, as fractions of persons only?

The South contended that black slaves were not
equal to white men as producers of wealth, and
that, by counting them as such, taxation would
be unequal and unjust. But whether counted as
units or as fractions of units, the slaveholders insisted that representation should be according to
that enumeration. The Northern reply was that,
if representation was to be according to population,
the slaves being included, then the slave States
would have a representation of property, for which
there would be no equivalent in States where there
were no slaves; but if slaves were enumerated as

[1] In some of the States slaves were reckoned as " chattels personal; " in others as " real estate."

a basis of representation, then that enumeration should also be taken to fix the rate of taxation.

Here, at any rate, was a basis for an interesting deadlock. One simple way out of it would have been to insist upon the doctrine of the civil law; to count the slaves only as *pro quadrupedibus*, to be left out of the enumeration of population as being no part of the State, as horses and cattle were left out. But the bonds of union hung loosely upon the sisters a hundred years ago; there was not one of them who did not think she was able to set up for herself and take her place among the nations as an independent sovereign; and it is more than likely that half of them would have refused to wear those bonds any longer on such a condition. There was no apprehension then that slavery was to become a power for evil in the State; but there was intense anxiety lest the States should fly asunder, form partial and local unions among neighbors, or become entangled in alliances with foreign nations, at the sacrifice of all, or much, that was gained by the Revolution. To make any concession, therefore, to slavery for the sake of the Union was hardly held to be a concession.

The curious student of history, however, who loves to study those problems of what might have happened if events that did not happen had come to pass, will find ample room for speculation in the possibilities of this one. Had there been no compromise, it is as easy to see now, as it was easy

to foresee then, how quickly the feeble bond of
union would have snapped asunder. But nevertheless, if the North had insisted that the slaves
should neither be counted nor represented at all,
or else should be reckoned in full and taxes levied
accordingly, the consequent dissolution of the Confederacy might have had consequences which then
nobody dreamed of. For it is not impossible, it
is not even improbable, that, in that event, the
year 1800 would have seen slavery in the process
of rapid extinction everywhere except in South
Carolina and Georgia. Had the event been postponed in those States to a later period, it would
only have been because they had already found in
the cultivation of indigo and rice a profitable use
for slave-labor, which did not exist in the other
slave States, where the supply of slaves was rapidly exceeding the demand. There can hardly be
a doubt that, in case of the dissolution of the Confederacy, the Northern free-labor States would
soon have consolidated into a strong union of their
own. There was every reason for hastening it,
and none so strong for hindering it as those which
were overborne in the union which was actually
formed soon afterward between the free-labor and
slave-labor States. To such a Northern union the
border States, as they sloughed off the old system,
would have been naturally attracted ; nor can
there be a doubt that a federal union so formed
would ultimately have proved quite as strong,
quite as prosperous, quite as happy, and quite as

respectable among the nations, as one purchased by compromises with slavery, followed, as those compromises were, by three quarters of a century of bitter political strife ending in a civil war.

But the Northern members were no less ready to make compromises than Southern members were to insist upon them, these no more understanding what they conceded than those understood what they gained; for the future was equally concealed from both. A committee reported that two blacks should be rated as one free man. This was unsatisfactory. To some it seemed too large, to others too small. Other ratios, therefore, were proposed, — three to one, three to two, four to one, and four to three. Mr. Madison at last, "in order," as he said, "to give a proof of the sincerity of his professions of liberality," — and doubtless he meant to be liberal, — proposed "that slaves should be rated as five to three." His motion was adopted, but afterward reconsidered. Four days later — April 1st — Mr. Hamilton renewed the proposition, and it was carried, Madison says, "without opposition." [1] The law on this point was the precedent for the mischievous three fifths rule of the Constitution adopted four years later.

[1] J. C. Hamilton says, in his *History of the Republic*, that " the motion prevailed by a vote of all the States excepting Massachusetts and Rhode Island." But his understanding of the question is in other respects incorrect, — misunderstood, one may hope, rather than misstated lest he should give credit, for what he considered a meritorious action, to Madison.

Youth finally overtook the young man during the last winter of his term in Congress, for he fell in love. But it was an unfortunate experience, and the outcome of it doubtless gave a more sombre hue than ever to his life. His choice was not a wise one. Probably Mr. Madison seemed a much older man than he really was at that period of his life, and to a young girl may have appeared really advanced in years. At any rate, it was his unhappy fate to be attached to a young lady of more than usual beauty and of irrepressible vivacity, — Miss Catherine Floyd, a daughter of General William Floyd of Long Island, N. Y., who was one of the signers of the Declaration of Independence, and who was a delegate to Congress from 1774 to 1783. Miss Catherine's sixteenth birthday was in April of the latter year; Madison was double her age, as his thirty-second birthday was a month earlier. His suit, however, was accepted, and they became engaged. But it was the father rather than the daughter who admired the suitor; for the older statesman better understood the character, and better appreciated the abilities, of his young colleague, and predicted a brilliant career for him. The girl's wisdom was of another kind. The future career which she foresaw and wanted to share belonged to a young clergyman, who — according to the reminiscences of an aged relative of hers — "hung round her at the harpsichord," and made love in quite another fashion than that of the

solemn statesman whom the old general so approved of. It is altogether a pretty love story, and
one's sympathy goes out to the lively young beauty,
who was thinking of love and not of ambition, as
she turned from the old young gentleman, discuss-
ing, with her wise father, the public debt and the
necessity of an impost, to that really young young
gentleman who knew how to hang over the harpsichord, and talked more to the purpose with his
eyes than ever the other could with his lips. There
is a tradition that she was encouraged to be thus
on with the new love before she was off with the
old, by a friend somewhat older than herself; and
possibly this maturer lady may have thought that
Madison would be better mated with one nearer his
own age. At any rate, the engagement was broken
off before long by the dismissal of the older lover,
much to the father's disappointment, and in due
time the young lady married the other suitor.
There is no reason that I know of for supposing
that she ever regretted that her more humble home
was in a rectory, when it might have been, in due
time, had she chosen differently, in the White
House at Washington, and that afterward she
might have lived, the remaining sixteen years of
her life, the honored wife of a revered ex-President.
Perhaps, however, she smiled in those later years
at the recollection of having laughed in her gay
and thoughtless youth at her solemn lover, and
that, when at last she dismissed him, she sealed her

letter — conveying to him alone, it may be, some merry but mischievous meaning — with a bit of rye-dough.[1]

Mr. Rives gives a letter from Jefferson to Madison at this time, which shows that he stood in need of consolation from his friends. " I sincerely lament," Mr. Jefferson wrote in his philosophical way, " the misadventure which has happened, from whatever cause it may have happened. Should it be final, however, the world presents the same and many other resources of happiness, and you possess many within yourself. Firmness of mind and unintermitting occupation will not long leave you in pain. No event has been more contrary to my expectations, and these were founded on what I thought a good knowledge of the ground. But of all machines ours is the most complicated and inexplicable." It was Solomon who said, " there be three things which are too wonderful for me, yea, four which I know not." This fourth was, " the way of a man with a maid." He might have added a fifth, — the way of a maid with a man, which, evidently, is what Jefferson meant.

[1] For the details, so far as they can now be recalled, of this single romantic incident in Mr. Madison's life, I am indebted to Nicoll Floyd, Esq., of Moriches, Long Island, a great-grandson of General William Floyd.

# CHAPTER IV

## IN THE STATE ASSEMBLY

As the election of the same delegate to Congress for consecutive sessions was then forbidden by the law of Virginia, Mr. Madison was not returned to that body in 1784. For a brief interval of three months he made good use of his time, we are told, by continuing his law studies, till in the spring of that year he was chosen to represent his county in the Virginia Assembly. It may be that " the sentiments and manners of the parent nation," which he lamented seven years before, had passed away, and nobody now insisted upon the privilege of getting drunk at the candidate's expense before voting for him. But it is more likely that the electors had not changed. The difference was in the candidate; they did not need to be allured to give their votes to a man whom they were proud to call upon to represent the county. Mr. Madison's reputation was already made by his three years in Congress, and he now easily took a place among the political leaders of his own State.

The position was hardly less conspicuous or less influential than that which he had held in the national Congress. What each State might do

was of quite as much importance as anything the
federal government might or could do.  Congress
could neither open nor close a single port in Virginia to commerce, whether domestic or foreign,
without the consent of the State ; it could not levy
a tax of a penny on anything, whether goods coming in or products going out, if the State objected.
As a member of Congress, Mr. Madison might propose or oppose any of these things ; as a member
of the Virginia House of Delegates, he might, if
his influence was strong enough, carry or forbid
any or all of them, whatever might be the wishes
of Congress.  It was in the power of Virginia to
influence largely the welfare of her neighbors, so
far as it depended upon commerce, and indirectly
that of every State in the Union.

In the Assembly, as in Congress, Mr. Madison's
aim was to increase the powers of the federal
government, for want of which it was rapidly sinking into imbecility and contempt.  " I acceded,"
he says, " to the desire of my fellow-citizens of
the county that I should be one of its representatives in the legislature," to bring about " a rescue
of the Union and the blessings of liberty staked
on it from an impending catastrophe."  Early in
the session the Assembly assented to the amendment to the Articles of Confederation proposed at
the late session of Congress, which substituted
population for a land valuation as the basis of representation and of taxation.  The Assembly also
asserted that all requisitions upon the States for

the support of the general government and to provide for the public debt should be complied with,
and payment of balances on old accounts should
be enforced; and it assented to the recommendation of Congress that that body should have power
for a limited period to control the trade with foreign nations having no treaty with the United
States, in order that it might retaliate upon Great
Britain for excluding American ships from her
West India colonies. All these measures were
designed for " the rescue of the Union," and they
had, of course, Madison's hearty support. For it
was absolutely essential, as he believed, that something should be done if the Union was to be saved,
or to be made worth saving. But there were
obstacles on all sides. The commercial States
were reluctant to surrender the control over trade
to Congress; in the planting States there was
hardly any trade that could be surrendered. In
Virginia the tobacco planter still clung to the old
ways. He liked to have the English ship take his
tobacco from the river bank of his own plantation,
and to receive from the same vessel such coarse
goods as were needed to clothe his slaves, with the
more expensive luxuries for his own family, — dry
goods for his wife and daughter; the pipe of madeira, the coats and breeches, the hats, boots, and
saddles for himself and his sons. He knew that
this year's crop went to pay — if it did pay — for
last year's goods, and that he was always in debt.
But the debt was on running account, and did not

matter.  The London factor was skillful in charges
for interest and commissions, and the account for
this year was always a lien on next year's crop.
He knew, and the planter knew, that the tobacco
could be sold at a higher price in New York ,or
Philadelphia than the factor got, or seemed to
get, for it in London ; that the goods sent out
in exchange were charged at a higher price than
they could be bought for in the Northern towns.
Nevertheless, the planter liked to see his own hogsheads rolled on board ship by his own negroes at
his own wharf, and receive in return his own boxes
and bales shipped direct from London at his own
order, let it cost what it might.  It was a shift-
less and ruinous system ; but the average Virginia
planter was not over-quick at figures, nor even at
reading and writing.  He was proud of being lord
of a thousand or two acres, and one or two hundred
negroes, and fancied that this was to rule over, as
Mr. Rives called it, "a mimic commonwealth, with
its foreign and domestic relations, and its regular
administrative hierarchy."  He did not comprehend that the isolated life of a slave plantation
was ordinarily only a kind of perpetual barbecue,
with its rough sports and vacuous leisure, where
the roasted ox was largely wasted and not always
pleasant to look at.  There was a rude hospitality,
where food, provided by unpaid labor, was cheap
and abundant, and where the host was always glad
to welcome any guest who would relieve him of his
own tediousness; but there was little luxury and

no refinement where there was almost no culture. Of course there were a few homes and families of another order, where the women were refined and the men educated ; but these were the exceptions. Society generally, with its bluff, loud, self-confident but ignorant planters, its numerous poor whites destitute of lands and of slaves, and its mass of slaves whose aim in life was to avoid work and escape the whip, was necessarily only one remove from semi-civilization.

It was not easy to indoctrinate such a people, more arrogant than intelligent, with new ideas. By the same token it might be possible to lead them into new ways before they would find out whither they were going. Mr. Madison hoped to change the wretched system of plantation commerce by a port bill, which he brought into the Assembly. Imposts require custom-houses, and obviously there could not be custom-houses nor even custom-officers on every plantation in the State. The bill proposed to leave open two ports of entry for all foreign ships. It would greatly simplify matters if all the foreign trade of the State could be limited to these two ports only. It would then be easy enough to enforce imposts, and the State would have something to surrender to the federal government to help it to a revenue, if, happily, the time should ever come when all the States should assent to that measure of salvation for the Union. Not that this was the primary object of those who favored this port law ; but the

question of commerce was the question on which
everything hinged, and its regulation in each State
must needs have an influence, one way or the other,
upon the possibility of strengthening, even of preserving, the Union. Everything depended upon
reconciling these state interests by mutual concessions. The South was jealous of the North, because trade flourished at the North and did not
flourish at the South. It seemed as if this was at
the expense of the South, and so, in a certain sense,
it was. The problem was to find where the difficulty lay, and to apply the remedy.

If commerce flourished at the North, where each
of the States had one or two ports of entry only,
why should it not flourish in Virginia if regulated
in the same way? If those centres of trade bred
a race of merchants, who built their own ships,
bought and sold, did their own carrying, competed
with and stimulated each other, and encroached
upon the trade of the South, why should not
similar results follow in Virginia if she should
confine her trade to two or three ports? If the
buyer and the seller, the importer and the con-
sumer, went to a common place of exchange in
Philadelphia, New York, and Boston, and prosperity followed as a consequence, why should they
not do the same thing at Norfolk? This was
what Madison aimed to bring about by the port
bill. But it was impossible to get it through the
legislature till three more ports were added to the
two which the bill at first proposed. When the

planters came to understand that such a law would
take away their cherished privilege of trade along
the banks of the rivers, wherever anybody chose to
run out a little jetty, the opposition was persistent.
At every succeeding session, till the new federal
Constitution was adopted, an attempt was made to
repeal the act; and though that was not successful,
each year new ports of entry were added. It did
not, indeed, matter much whether the open ports
of Virginia were two or whether they were twenty.
There was a factor in the problem which neither
Mr. Madison nor anybody else would take into the
account. It was possible, of course, if force enough
were used, to break up the traffic with English
ships on the banks of the rivers; but when that
was done, commerce would follow its own laws, in
spite of the acts of the legislature, and flow into
channels of its own choosing. It was not possible
to transmute a planting State, where labor was
enslaved, into a commercial State, where labor
must be free.

However desirous Mr. Madison might be to
transfer the power over commerce to the federal
government, he was compelled, as a member of the
Virginia legislature, to care first for the trade of
his own State. No State could afford to neglect
its own commercial interests so long as the thirteen
States remained thirteen commercial rivals. It
was becoming plainer and plainer every day that,
while that relation continued, the less chance there
was that thirteen petty, independent States could

unite into one great nation. No foreign power
would make a treaty with a government which
could not enforce that treaty among its own people.
Neither could any separate portion of that people
make a treaty, as any other portion, the other side
of an imaginary line, need not hold it in respect.
What good was there in revenue laws, or, indeed,
in any other laws in Massachusetts which Connecticut and Rhode Island disregarded? or in New
York, if New Jersey and Pennsylvania laughed at
them? or in Virginia, if Maryland held them in
contempt?

But Mr. Madison felt that, if he could bring
about a healthful state of things in the trade of
his own State, there was at least so much done
towards bringing about a healthful state of things
in the commerce of the whole country. There
came up a practical, local question which, when
the time came, he was quick to see had a logical
bearing upon the general question. The Potomac was the boundary line between Virginia and
Maryland; but Lord Baltimore's charter gave to
Maryland jurisdiction over the river to the Virginia bank; and this right Virginia had recognized, claiming only for herself the free navigation
of the Potomac and the Pocomoke. Of course the
laws of neither State were regarded when it was
worth while to evade them; and nothing was easier
than to evade them, since to the average human
mind there is no privilege so precious as a facility
for smuggling. Nobody, at any rate, seems to have

thought anything about the matter till it came
under Madison's observation after his return home
from Congress.  To him it meant something more
than mere evasion of state laws and frauds on the
state revenue.  The subject fell into line with his
reflections upon the looseness of the bonds that
held the States together, and how unlikely it was
that they would ever grow into a respectable or
prosperous nation while their present relations
continued.  Virtually there was no maritime law
on the Potomac, and hardly even the pretense of
any.   What could be more absurd than to provide
ports of entry on one bank of a river, while on the
other bank, from the source to the sea, the whole
country was free to all comers?  If the laws of
either State were to be regarded on the opposite
bank, a treaty was as necessary between them as
between any two contiguous states in Europe.

Madison wrote to Jefferson, who was now a
delegate in Congress, pointing out this anomalous
condition of things on the Potomac, and suggest-
ing that he should confer with the Maryland delegates upon the subject.  The proposal met with
Jefferson's approbation ; he sought an interview
with Mr. Stone, a delegate from Maryland, and,
as he wrote to Madison, "finding him of the same
opinion, [I] have told him I would, by letters,
bring the subject forward on our part.  They will
consider it, therefore, as originated by this conversation."  Why " they " should not have been
permitted to " consider it as originated " from

Madison's suggestion that Jefferson should have such a conversation is not quite plain; for it was Madison, not Jefferson, who had discovered that here was a wrong that ought to be righted, and who had proposed that each State should appoint commissioners to look into the matter and apply a remedy. So, also, so far as subsequent negotiation on this subject had any influence in bringing about the Constitutional Convention of 1787, it was only because Mr. Madison, having suggested the first practical step in the one case, seized an opportune moment in that negotiation to suggest a similar practical step in the other case. As it is so often said that the Annapolis Convention of 1786 was the direct result of the discussion of the Potomac question, it is worth while to explain what they really had to do with each other.

The Virginia commissioners were appointed early in the session on Mr. Madison's motion. Maryland moved more slowly, and it was not till the spring of 1785 that the commissioners met. They soon found that any efficient jurisdiction over the Potomac involved more interests than they, or those who appointed them, had considered. Existing difficulties might be disposed of by agreeing upon uniform duties in the two States, and this the commissioners recommended. But when the subject came before the Maryland legislature it took a wider range.

The Potomac Company, of which Washington was president, had been chartered only a few months before. The work it proposed to do was to make the upper Potomac navigable, and to connect it by a good road with the Ohio River. This was to encourage the settlement of Western lands. Another company was chartered about the same time to connect the Potomac and Delaware by a canal, where interstate traffic would be more immediate. Pennsylvania and Delaware must necessarily have a deep interest in both these projects, and the Maryland legislature proposed that those States be invited to appoint commissioners to act with those whom Maryland and Virginia had already appointed to settle the conflict between them upon the question of jurisdiction on the Potomac. Then it occurred to somebody : if four States can confer, why should not thirteen ? The Maryland legislature thereupon suggested that all the States be invited to send delegates to a convention to take up the whole question of American commerce.

While this was going on in Maryland, the Virginia legislature was considering petitions from the principal ports of the State praying that some remedy might be devised for the commercial evils from which they were all suffering. The port bill had manifestly proved a failure. It was only a few weeks before that Madison had complained, in a letter to a friend, that " the trade of the country is in a most deplorable condition ; " that the most " shameful frauds " were committed by the English merchants upon those in Virginia, as well

as upon the planters who shipped their own tobacco; that the difference in the price of tobacco
at Philadelphia and in Virginia was from eleven
shillings to fourteen shillings in favor of the
Northern ports; and that " the price of merchandise here is, at least, as much above, as that of tobacco is below, the Northern standard." He was
only the more confirmed in his opinion that there
was no cure for these radical evils except to surrender to the confederate government complete
control over commerce. The debate upon these
petitions was hot and long. It brought out the
strongest men on both sides, Madison leading
those who wished to give to Congress the power
to regulate trade with foreign countries when no
treaty existed; to make uniform commercial laws
for all the States; and to levy an impost of five
per cent. on imported merchandise, as a provision
for the public debt and for the support of the
federal government generally. A committee, of
which he was a member, at length reported instructions to the delegates of the State in Congress to
labor for the consent of all the States to these propositions. But in Committee of the Whole the
resolutions were so changed and qualified — especially in limiting to thirteen years the period for
which Congress was to be intrusted with a power
so essential to the existence of the government —
that the measure was given up by its friends as
hopeless.

But before the report was disposed of Mr. Madison prepared a resolution, to be offered as a substitute, with the hope of reaching the same end in another way. This resolution provided for the appointment of five commissioners, — Madison to be one of them, — " who, or any three of whom, shall meet such commissioners as may be appointed in the other States of the Union, at a time and place to be agreed on, to take into consideration the trade of the United States; to examine the relative situations and trade of said States ; to consider how far a uniform system in their commercial regulations may be necessary to their common interest and their permanent harmony; and to report to the several States such an act, relative to this great object, as, when unanimously ratified by them, will enable the United States, in Congress, effectually to provide for the same." This he was careful not to offer himself, but, as he says, it was " introduced by Mr. Tyler, an influential member, who, having never served in Congress, had more the ear of the House than those whose services there exposed them to an imputable bias." He adds that " it was so little acceptable that it was not then persisted in."

About the same time the action of the Maryland legislature on the Potomac question, and the report of the Potomac commissioners, came up for consideration. Mr. Madison said afterward that, as Maryland thought the concurrence of Pennsylvania and Delaware were necessary to the regulation of trade on that river, so those States would, proba-

bly, wish to ask for the concurrence of their neighbors in any proposed arrangement. "So apt and
forcible an illustration," he adds, " of the necessity
of an uniformity throughout all the States could
not but favor the passage of a resolution which
proposed a convention having that for its object."

As one of the Potomac commissioners, he knew,
of course, what was coming from Maryland, and
"how apt and forcible an illustration" it would
seem, when it did come, of that resolution which
he had written and had induced Mr. Tyler to offer.
It did not matter that the resolution had been at
the moment "so little acceptable," and therefore
"not then persisted in." It was where it was sure,
in the political slang of our day, to do the most
good. And so it came about. All that Maryland
had proposed, growing out of the consideration
of the Potomac question, the Virginia legislature
acceded to. Then, on the last day of the session,
the Madison-Tyler resolution was taken from the
table, where it had lain quietly for nearly two
months, and passed. If some, who had been contending all winter against any action which should
lead to a possibility of strengthening the federal
government, failed to see how important a step
they had taken to that very end; if any, who
were fearful of federal usurpation and tenacious of
state rights, were blind to the fact that the resolution had pushed aside the Potomac question and
put the Union question in its place, Mr. Madison,
we may be sure, was not one of that number. He

had gained that for which he had been striving for years.

The commissioners appointed by the resolution soon came together. They appointed Annapolis as the place, and the second Monday of the following September (1786) as the time, of the proposed national convention; and they sent to all the other States an invitation to send delegates to that convention.

On September 11 commissioners from Virginia, Delaware, Pennsylvania, New Jersey, and New York assembled at Annapolis. Others had been appointed by North Carolina, Rhode Island, Massachusetts, and New Hampshire, but they were not present. Georgia, South Carolina, Maryland, and Connecticut had taken no action upon the subject. As five States only were represented, the commissioners " did not conceive it advisable to proceed on the business of their mission," but they adopted an address, written by Alexander Hamilton, to be sent to all the States.

All the represented States, the address said, had authorized their commissioners " to take into consideration the trade and commerce of the United States; to consider how far an uniform system in their commercial intercourse and regulations might be necessary to their common interest and permanent harmony." But New Jersey had gone farther than this; her delegates were instructed " to consider how far an uniform system in their commercial regulations *and other important matters* might be necessary to the common interest and permanent harmony of the several States." This, the commissioners present thought, " was an improvement on the original plan, and will deserve to be incorporated into that of a future convention." They gave their reasons at length for this opinion, and, in conclusion, urged that commissioners from all the States be appointed to meet in convention at Philadelphia on the second Monday of the following May (1787), "to devise such further provisions as shall appear to them necessary to render the Constitution of the federal government adequate to the exigencies of the Union."

In the course of the winter delegates to this convention were chosen by the several States. Virginia was the first to choose her delegates; Madison was among them, and at their head was George Washington.

# CHAPTER V

## IN THE VIRGINIA LEGISLATURE

THAT the Annapolis Convention ever met to make smooth the way for the more important one which came together eight months afterward and framed a permanent Constitution for the United States was unquestionably due to the persistence and the political adroitness of Mr. Madison. But it was not exceptional work. The same diligence and devotion to public duty mark the whole of this period of three years through which he continued a member of the state legislature. As chairman of the judiciary committee he reduced with much labor the old colonial statutes to a body of laws befitting the condition of free citizens in an independent State. From his first to his last session he contended, though without success, for the faith of treaties and the honest payment of debts. The treaty with England provided that there should be "no lawful impediment on either side to the recovery of debts heretofore contracted." The legislature notified Congress that it should disregard this provision, on the plea that in relation to "slaves and other property" it had not been observed by Great Britain. Mr.

Madison did not then know that — as he said three
years later — " the infractions [of the treaty] on
the part of the United States preceded even the
violation on the other side in the instance of the
negroes." He maintained, nevertheless, that the
settlement of the difficulty, if it had any real
foundation, belonged to Congress, the party to the
treaty, and not to a State which had surrendered
the treaty-making power; and that in common
honesty one planter was not relieved from his
obligation to pay a London merchant for goods
and merchandise received before the war, because
other planters had not been paid for the negroes
and horses they had lost when the British troops
invaded Virginia. At each of the three sessions
of the legislature, while he was a member, he
tried to bring that body to adopt some line of
conduct which should not — to use his own words
— " extremely dishonor us and embarrass Congress." It was useless; the repudiators were
quite deaf to any appeals either to their honor
or their patriotism.

On another question both he and his State were
more fortunate. Religious freedom had to be once
more fought for, and he was quick to come to the
defense of a right which had first called forth his
youthful enthusiasm. Two measures were brought
forward from session to session to secure for the
church the support of the state. The first was a
bill for the incorporation of religious societies;
but when it was pushed to its final passage it pro-

vided for the incorporation of Episcopal churches only.  For this Mr. Madison consented to vote, though with reluctance, in the hope that the church party would be so far satisfied with this measure as to abstain from pushing another which was still more objectionable.

He was disappointed.  Naturally those who had carried their first point were the more, not the less, anxious for further success.  Now it was insisted that there should be a universal tax "for the support of teachers of the Christian religion." The tax-payer was to be permitted to name the religious society for the support of which he preferred to contribute.  If he declined this voluntary acquiescence in the law, the money would be used in aid of a school ; but from the tax itself none were to be exempt on any pretext.  Madison was quick to see in such a law the possibility of religious intolerance, of compulsory uniformity enforced by the civil power, and of the suppression of any freedom of conscience or opinion. The act did not define who were and who were not "teachers of the Christian religion," and that necessarily would be left to the courts to decide. A state church would be the inevitable consequence ; for it was not to be supposed that any dominant sect would rest till it secured the recognition by law of its own denomination as the sole representative of the Christian religion.  To expect anything else was to ignore the teachings of all history.

The burden of opposition and debate fell, at
first, almost solely upon Madison. Some of the
wisest and best men of the State were slow to see,
as he saw, that religious freedom was in danger
from such legislation. There was, it was said, a
sad falling-off in public morality as indifference
to religion increased. There was no cure, it was
declared, for prevalent and growing corruption
except in the culture of the religious sentiment,
and the teachers of religion, therefore, must be
upheld and supported. But granting all this,
Madison saw that the proposed remedy would be
to give, not bread but a stone, and a stone that
would be used in return as a weapon. It was
impossible to regulate religious belief by act of the
Assembly, and therefore it was worse than foolish
to try.

It was due to him that the question was postponed from one session to the next. A copy of
the bill was sent, meanwhile, into every county
of the State for the consideration of the people,
and that was aided by a " Memorial and Remonstrance," written by Madison, which was circulated
everywhere for signature, in readiness for presentation to the next legislature. The bill, the memorial said, would be " a dangerous abuse of power,"
and the signers protested against it with unanswerable arguments, taking for a starting-point the
assertion of the Bill of Rights, " that religion, or
the duty we owe to our Creator, and the manner
of discharging it, can be directed only by reason

and conviction, not by force or violence." It is
not at all improbable that many signed this remonstrance, not so much because they believed it to
be true as because it was a protest against a tax;
that others were more moved by jealousy of the
power of the Episcopal Church than they were by
anxiety to protect religious liberty outside of their
own sects. But whatever the motives, the movement was too formidable to be disregarded. It
was made a test question in the election of members for the legislature of 1785–86; at that session
the bill for the support of religious teachers was
rejected, and in place of it was passed " an act for
establishing religious freedom," written by Jefferson seven years before. This provided " that no
man shall be compelled to frequent or support any
religious worship, place, or ministry whatsoever,
nor shall be enforced, restrained, molested, or
burthened in his body or goods, nor shall otherwise suffer on account of his religious opinions or
belief; but that all men shall be free to profess,
and by argument maintain, their opinions in matters of religion, and that the same shall in no
wise diminish, enlarge, or affect their civil capaci-
ties." [1]

[1] With how much interest Jefferson watched the progress of this
controversy he showed in his letters from Paris. In February,
1786, he wrote to Madison: " I thank you for the communication of the remonstrance against the assessment. Mazzei, who is
now in Holland, promised me to have it published in the *Leyden
Gazette*. It will do us great honor. I wish it may be as much
approved by our Assembly as by the wisest part of Europe."

In the memorial and remonstrance Madison had said: "If this freedom be abused, it is an offense against God, not against man. To God, therefore, not to man, must an account of it be rendered." If the people of Virginia did not clearly comprehend this doctrine in all its length and breadth a hundred years ago, it is not quite easy to say who were then, or who are now, at liberty to throw stones at them. The assertion of the broadest religious freedom was no more new then than it is true that persecution for opinion's sake is now only an ancient evil. It was not till fifty years after Virginia had refused to tax her citizens for the support of religious teachers that Massachusetts repealed the law that had long imposed a similar burden upon her people.

It was in 1786, the last year of Madison's ser-

Again, in December of the same year, he says: "The Virginia Act for religious freedom has been received with infinite approbation in Europe, and propagated with enthusiasm. I do not mean by the governments, but by the individuals who compose them. It has been translated into French and Italian, has been sent to most of the courts of Europe, and has been the best evidence of the falsehood of those reports which stated us to be in anarchy. It is inserted in the *Encyclopédie*, and is appearing in most of the publications respecting America. In fact, it is comfortable to see the standard of reason at length erected, after so many ages, during which the human mind had been held in vassalage by kings, priests, and nobles; and it is honorable for us to have produced the first legislature who had the courage to declare that the reason of man may be trusted with the formation of his own opinions!" This latter passage is characteristic, and many who do not like Jefferson will read between the lines the exultation of a man who was not always careful to draw the line between religious liberty and irreligious license.

vice in the Virginia Assembly before he returned
to Congress, that the craze of paper money broke
out again through all the States. The measure
was carried in most of them, followed in the end
by the usual disastrous consequences. Madison's
anxiety was great lest his own State should be
carried away by this delusion, and he led the opposition against some petitions sent to the Assembly
praying for an issue of currency. The vote against
it was too large to be due altogether to his influence ; but he gave great strength and concentration
to the opposition. In Virginia, tobacco certificates
supplied in some measure the want of a circulat-
ing medium, and it was, therefore, easier there
than in some of the other States to resist the
clamor for a paper substitute for real money. A
tobacco certificate at least represented something
worth money. Madison assented to a bill which
authorized the use of such certificates. But his
"acquiescence," he wrote to Washington, "was
extorted by a fear that some greater evil, under
the name of relief to the people, would be substituted." He was "far from being sure," he
added, that he "did right." But no evils with
which he had to reproach himself followed that
measure.

These three years of his life were probably
among the happiest, if they were not altogether
the happiest, in his long public career. There was
little disappointment or anxiety, and evidently
much genuine satisfaction as he saw how certainly

he was gaining a high place in the estimation of
his fellow-citizens for his devotion to the best
interests of his native State. In the recesses of
the legislature he had leisure for studies in which
he evidently found great contentment. He traveled a good deal at intervals, especially at the
North; learned much of the resources and character of the people outside of Virginia, and became
acquainted with the leading men among them.
Jefferson urged him to pass a summer with him in
Paris; and some foreign diplomatic service was
open to him, had he expressed a willingness to
accept it. But he preferred to know something
more of his own country while he had the leisure;
and if his life was to be passed in public service,
as now seemed probable to him, he chose, at least
for the present, to serve his country at home,
where he thought he was more needed, rather than
abroad. In his orders for books sent to Jefferson
the direction of his studies is evident. He sought
largely for those which treated of the science of
government; but they were not confined to that
subject. Natural history had great charms for
him. He was a diligent student of Buffon, and
was anxious to find, if possible, the plates of his
thirty-one volumes, in colors, that he might adorn
the walls of his room with them. He made careful
comparisons between the animals of other conti-
nents, as described and portrayed by the naturalist,
and similar orders in America. All new inventions
interested him. " I am so pleased," he writes,

"with the new invented lamp that I shall not grudge two guineas for one of them." He had seen "a pocket compass of somewhat larger diameter than a watch, and which may be carried in the same way. It has a spring for stopping the vibration of the needle when not in use. One of these would be very convenient in case of a ramble into the western country." A small telescope, he suggests, might be fitted on as a handle to a cane, which might "be a source of many little gratifications," when "in walks for exercise or amusement objects present themselves which it might be matter of curiosity to inspect, but which it was difficult or impossible to approach." Jefferson writes him of a new invention, a pedometer; and he wants one for his own pocket. Trifles like these show the bent of his mind; and they show a contented mind as well.

While writing of important acts of the legislature of 1785, he is careful to give other information in a letter to Jefferson, which is not uninteresting as written ninety-eight years ago, and written by him.

"I. Rumsey," he says, "by a memorial to the last session, represented that he had invented a mechanism by which a boat might be worked with little labor, at the rate of from twenty-five to forty miles a day, against a stream running at the rate of ten miles an hour, and prayed that the disclosure of his invention might be purchased by the public. The apparent extravagance of his pretensions brought a ridicule upon them, and nothing was done. In the recess of the Assembly he exemplified his machinery to General Washington and a few other gentlemen, who gave a certificate of the reality and importance of the invention, which opened the ears of this Assembly to a second memorial. The act gives a monopoly for ten years, reserving a right to abolish it at any time by paying £10,000. The inventor is soliciting similar acts from other States, and will not, I suppose, publish the secret till he either obtains or despairs of them."

This intelligence was evidently not unheeded by Jefferson. In writing, some months after he received it, to a friend on the application of steam-power to grist-mills, then lately introduced in England, he adds : " I hear you are applying the same agent in America to navigate boats, and I have little doubt but that it will be applied generally to machines, so as to supersede the use of water-ponds, and of course to lay open all the streams for navigation." Nor does Madison seem to have been one of those who doubted if anything was to come of Rumsey's invention. All this was less than a hundred years ago, and now there is a steam-ferry between New York and Europe running about twice a day.

In a similar letter, a year later, he is careful, among grave political matters, to remember and report to the same friend that in the sinking of a well in Richmond, on the declivity of a hill, there had been found, " about seventy feet below the surface, several large bones, apparently belonging to a fish not less than the shark ; and, what is more singular, several fragments of potter's ware in the style of the Indians. Before he [the digger] reached these curiosities he passed through about fifty feet of soft blue clay." Mr. Madison had only just heard of this discovery, and he had not seen the unearthed fragments. But he evidently accepts the story as true in coming from " unexceptionable witnesses." He adds, as a corroboration, that he is told by a friend from Washington County of the finding there, in the sinking of a salt-well, " of the hip-bone of the incognitum, the socket of which was about eight inches in diameter." Such things were peculiarly interesting to Jefferson, and Madison was too devoted a friend to him to leave them unnoticed. But they were hardly less interesting to himself, though he had not much of Jefferson's habit of scientific investigation. That " the potter's ware in the style of the Indians " should be found so deeply buried only seems to him " singular ; " nor, indeed, is there any record, so far as we know, that this particular fact was any more suggestive to Jefferson, though apparently so likely to arouse his inquiring mind to seek for some satisfactory explanation. But his geological notions were too positive to admit even of a doubt as to the age of man. Supposing a Creator, he assumed that " he created the earth at once, nearly in the state in which we see it, fit for the preservation of the beings he placed on it." Theorist as he was himself, he had little patience

with the other theorists who were already beginning to discover in the structure of the earth the
evidence of successive geological eras. The different strata of rocks and their inclination gave him
no trouble. He explained them all by the assumption that "rock grows, and it seems that it grows
in layers in every direction, as the branches of
trees grow in all directions." That evidences of
the existence of man should be found with a super-
imposed weight of earth seventy feet in thickness
would present to him no difficulty. If the fact
had specially aroused his attention he would have
explained it in some ingenious way as the result of
accident.

# CHAPTER VI

In February, 1787, Madison again took a seat in Congress. It was an anxious period. Shays's rebellion in Massachusetts had assumed rather formidable possibilities, and seemed not unlikely to spread to other States. Till this storm should blow over, the important business of Congress was to raise money and troops; in reality, to go to the help of Massachusetts, if need should be, though the object ostensibly was to protect a handful of people on the frontier against the Indians. It was a striking instance of the imbecility of the government under the Articles of Confederation, that it could only undertake to suppress rebellion in a State under the pretense of doing something else which came within the law. Massachusetts, it is true, was quite able to deal with her insurgents; but when Congress convened it was not known in New York that Lincoln had dispersed the main body of them at Petersham. Nevertheless, a like difficulty might arise at any moment in any other of the States, where the strength to meet it might be quite inadequate.

Madison's ideal still was, the Union before the

States, and for the sake of the States; the whole
before the parts, to save the parts; the binding
the fagot together that the sticks might not be lost.
" Our situation," he wrote to Edmund Randolph
in February, " is becoming every day more and
more critical.  No money comes into the federal
treasury; no respect is paid to the federal authority; and people of reflection unanimously agree
that the existing Confederacy is tottering to its
foundation.  Many individuals of weight, particularly in the eastern district, are suspected of leaning toward monarchy.  Other individuals predict
a partition of the States into two or more confederacies.  It is pretty certain that if some radical
amendment of the single one cannot be devised and
introduced, one or the other of these revolutions,
the latter no doubt, will take place."

It is not impossible that Madison himself may
have had some faith in this suspicion that " individuals of weight in the eastern district " were
inclined to a monarchy.  For such suspicion, however, there could be little real foundation.  There
were, doubtless, men of weight who thought and
said that monarchy was better than anarchy.
There were, doubtless, impatient men then who
thought and said, as there are impatient men now
who think and say, that the rule of a king is better
than the rule of the people.  But there was no dis-
loyalty to government by the people among those
who only maintained that the English in America
must draw from the common heritage of English

institutions and English law the material where-
with to build up the foundations of a new nation.
No intelligent and candid man doubts now that
they were wise; nor would it have been long
doubted then, had it not so speedily become manifest that, if the stigma of " British" was once
affixed to a political party, any appeal from popular prejudice to reason and common sense was
hopeless.

There were a few persons who would have done
away with the divisions of States and establish
in their place a central government. Those most
earnest in maintaining the autonomy of States
declared that such a government was, as Luther
Martin of Maryland called it, of " a monarchical
nature." What else could that be but a monarchy? An insinuation took on the form of a
logical deduction and became a popular fallacy.
Yet those most earnest for a central government
only sought to establish a stable rule in place of
no rule at all; or, worse still, of the tyranny of
an ignorant and vicious mob under the outraged
name of democracy, into which there was danger of
drifting. Whether their plan was wise or foolish,
it did not mean a monarchy. Even of Shays's
misguided followers Jefferson said : " I believe you
may be assured that an idea or desire of returning
to anything like their ancient government never
entered into their heads." As Madison knew and
said, the real danger was that the States would
divide into two confederacies, and only by a new

and wiser and stronger union could that calamity be averted.

To gain the assent of most of the States to a convention was surmounting only the least of the difficulties. Three weeks before the time of meeting Madison wrote: " The nearer the crisis approaches, the more I tremble for the issue. The necessity of gaining the concurrence of the convention in some system that will answer the purpose, the subsequent approbation of Congress, and the final sanction of the States, present a series of chances which would inspire despair in any case where the alternative was less formidable." He said, in the first month of the session of that body, that " the States were divided into different interests, not by their difference of size, but by other circumstances; the most material of which resulted partly from climate, but principally from the effects of their having or not having slaves. These two causes concurred in forming the great division of interests in the United States. It did not lie between the large and small States. It lay between the Northern and Southern."

During the earlier weeks of this session of Congress, and, indeed, for some months before, events had made so manifest this difference of interest, coincident with the difference in latitude, that there seemed little ground for hope that any good would come out of a constitutional convention. The old question of the navigation of the Mississippi was again agitated. The South held her

right to that river to be of much more value than
anything she could gain by a closer union with the
North, and she was quite ready to go to war with
Spain in defense of it. On the other hand, the
Northern States were quite indifferent to the navigation of the Mississippi, and not disposed apparently to make any exertion or sacrifice to secure
it. Just now they were anxious to secure a commercial treaty with Spain; but Spain insisted, as
a preliminary condition, that the United States
should relinquish all claim to navigation upon a
river whose mouths were within Spanish territory.
In the Northern mind there was no doubt of the
value of trade with Spain; and there was a good
deal of doubt whether there was anything worth
contending for in the right to sail upon a river
running through a wilderness where, as yet, there
were few inhabitants, and hardly any trade worth
talking about. More than that, there was unquestionably a not uncommon belief at the North
and East that the settlement and prosperity of the
West would be at the expense of the Atlantic
States. Perhaps that view of the matter was not
loudly insisted upon; but many were none the less
persuaded that, if population was attracted west-
ward by the hope of acquiring rich and cheap
lands, prosperity and power would go with it. At
any rate, those of this way of thinking were not
inclined to forego a certain good for that which
would profit them nothing, and might do them
lasting harm.

For these reasons, spoken and unspoken, the Northern members of Congress were at first quite willing, for the sake of a commercial treaty, to concede to Spain the exclusive control of the Mississippi. But to pacify the South it was proposed that the concession to Spain should be for only five and twenty years. If at the end of that period the navigation of the Mississippi should be worth contending for, the question could be reopened. The South was, of course, rather exasperated than pacified by such a proposition. The navigation of the river had not only a certain value to them now, but it was theirs by right, and that was reason enough for not parting with it even for a limited period. Concessions now would make the reassertion of the right the more difficult by and by. If it must be fought for, it would lessen the chance of success to put off the fighting five and twenty years. Indeed, it could not be put off, for war was already begun in a small way. The Spaniards had seized American boats on trading voyages down the river, and the Americans had retaliated upon some petty Spanish settlements. Spain, moreover, seemed at first no more inclined to listen to compromise than the South was.

England watched this controversy with interest. She had no expectation of recovering for herself the Floridas, which she had lost in the war of the Revolution, and had finally ceded to Spain by the treaty of 1783; but she was quite willing to see that power get into trouble on the Mississippi

question, and more than willing that it should
threaten the peace and union of the States. Her
own boundary line west of the Alleghanies might
possibly be extended far south of the Great Lakes,
if the Northern and Southern States should divide
into two confederacies; but, apart from any lust
of territory, she rejoiced at anything that threatened to check the growth of her late colonies.

Fortunately, however, the question was disposed
of, before the Constitutional Convention met at
Philadelphia, by the failure to secure a treaty.
The Spanish minister, Guardoqui, consented, at
length, after long resistance, to accept as a compromise the navigation of the river for five and
twenty years; but Mr. Jay, who was willing, could
he have had his way, to concede anything, found
at that stage of the negotiations he could not command votes enough in Congress to secure a treaty
even in that modified form. Hitherto he had
relied upon a resolution passed by Congress in
August, 1786, by the vote of seven Northern States
against five Southern. This, it was assumed,
repealed a resolution of the year before, and authorized the secretary to make a treaty. The resolution of the year before, August, 1785, had been
passed by the votes of nine States, and was in
confirmation of a provision of the Articles of Confederation declaring that " no treaties with foreign
powers should be entered into but by the assent of
nine States." The minority contended that such
a resolution could not be repealed by the vote of

only seven States, for that would be to violate a
fundamental condition of the Articles of Confederation. It is easy to see now that there ought not
to have been a difference among honorable men on
such a point as that. Nevertheless Mr. Jay, supported by some of the strongest Northern men,
held that the votes of seven States could be made,
in a roundabout way, to authorize an act which the
Constitution declared should never be lawful except
with the assent of nine States. So the secretary
went on with his negotiations and came to terms
with the Spanish minister.

In April the secretary was called upon to report
to Congress what was the position of these negotiations. Then it first publicly appeared that a
treaty was actually agreed upon which gave up the
right to the Mississippi for a quarter of a century.
But it was also speedily made plain by various
parliamentary motions that the seven votes, which
the friends of such a treaty had relied upon, had
fallen from seven — even could that number in
the end have been of use — to, at best, four. The
New Jersey delegates had been instructed not to
consent to the surrender of the American right to
the use of the Mississippi ; a new delegate from
Pennsylvania had changed the vote of that State ;
and Rhode Island had also gone over to the other
side. "It was considered, on the whole," wrote
Madison, "that the project for shutting the Mississippi was at an end."

These details are not unimportant. Forty-five

years afterward Madison wrote that "his main object, in returning to Congress at this time, was to bring about, if possible, the canceling of Mr. Jay's project for shutting the Mississippi." Probably it had occurred to nobody then that within less than twenty years the Province of Louisiana would belong to the United States, when their right to the navigation of the river could be no longer disputed. But so long as both its banks from the thirty-first degree of latitude southward to the Gulf remained foreign territory, it was of the last importance to the Southern States, whose territory extended to the Mississippi, that the right of way should not be surrendered. If a treaty with Spain could be carried that gave up this right, and the Southern States should be compelled to choose between the loss of the Mississippi and the loss of the Union, there could be little doubt as to what their choice would be. It was not a question to be postponed till after the Philadelphia Convention had convened; if not disposed of before, the convention might as well not meet.

Madison's letters, while the question was pending, show great anxiety. He was glad to know that the South was of one mind on this subject and would not yield an inch. He was quite confident that his own State would take the lead, as she soon did, in the firm avowal of Southern opinion. But he rejoiced that the question did not come up in the Virginia legislature till after the act was passed to send delegates to the Philadelphia Convention.

That he looked upon as a point gained, and the
delegates were presently appointed ; but he still
despaired of any good coming of the convention,
unless " Mr. Jay's project for shutting the Mississippi " could be first got rid of.

In a recent work [1] Mr. Madison is represented
as having " struck a bargain " with the Kentucky
delegates to the Virginia Assembly, agreeing to
speak on behalf of a petition relating to the Mississippi question, provided the delegates from Kentucky — then a part of Virginia — would vote
for the representation of Virginia at Philadelphia.
A " bargain " implies an exchange of one thing
for another, and Madison had no convictions in
favor of closing the Mississippi to exchange for a
service rendered on behalf of a measure for which
he wished to secure votes. Moreover, no bargain
was necessary. It was not easy to find anybody
in Virginia who needed to be persuaded that the
right to the Mississippi must not be surrendered.
Madison wrote to Monroe in October, 1786, that
it would " be defended by the legislature with as
much zeal as could be wished. Indeed, the only
danger is that too much resentment may be indulged by many against the federal councils." His
only apprehension was lest the Mississippi question should come up in the Assembly before the
report from the Annapolis Convention should be
disposed of, for if that were accepted the appoint-

---

[1] *A History of the People of the United States.* Vol. i. By John
Bach McMaster.

ment of delegates to Philadelphia was assured.
" I hope," he wrote to Washington in November,
" the report will be called for before the business
of the Mississippi begins to ferment." It happened as he wished. " The recommendation from
Annapolis," he wrote again a week later, " in favor
of a general revision of the federal system was
*unanimously* agreed to " (the emphasis is his own).
He afterward reported to Jefferson " that the project for bartering the Mississippi to Spain was
brought before the Assembly after the preceding
measure had been adopted." There was neither
delay nor difficulty in securing the unanimous consent of the Assembly to resolutions instructing the
members of Congress to oppose any concession
to Spain. But Madison's anxiety was not in the
least relieved by the speedy appointment of delegates to the Philadelphia Convention; for, he
wrote presently to Washington, " I am entirely
convinced, from what I observe here (at Richmond), that, unless the project of Congress can
be reversed, the hopes of carrying this State into
a proper federal system will be demolished." He
had already said, in the same letter, that the
resolutions on the Mississippi question had been
" agreed to unanimously in the House of Delegates," and three days before the letter was
written the delegates to Philadelphia had been
appointed.

# CHAPTER VII

## THE CONSTITUTIONAL CONVENTION

MR. MADISON is called "the Father of the Constitution." A paper written by him was laid before his colleagues of Virginia, before the meeting of the Constitutional Convention at Philadelphia, and was made the basis of the "Virginia plan," as it was called, out of which the Constitution was evolved. In another way his name is so identified with it that one cannot be forgotten so long as the other is remembered. From that full and faithful report of the proceedings of the convention, in which his own part was so active and conspicuous, we know most that we do or ever can know of the perplexities and trials, the concessions and triumphs, the acts of wisdom and the acts of weakness, of that body of men whose coming together time has shown to have been one of the important events in the history of mankind.

Then it is also true that no man had worked harder, perhaps none had worked so hard, to bring the public mind to a serious consideration of affairs and a recognition of the necessity of reorganizing the government, if the States were to be held together. Never, it seemed, had men better reason

to be satisfied with the result of their labors when,
a few months later, the new Constitution was
accepted by all the States.  Yet the time was not
far distant when even Madison would be in doubt
as to the character of this new bond of union, and
as to what sort of government had been secured by
it.  Nor till he had been dead near thirty years
was it to be determined what union under the
Constitution really meant; nor till three quarters
of a century after the adoption of that instrument
was the more perfect union formed, justice established, domestic tranquillity insured, the general
welfare promoted, and the blessings of liberty
secured to all the people, which by that great
charter it was intended, in 1787, to ordain and
establish.  All the difficulties, which they who
framed it escaped by their work, were as nothing
to those which it entailed upon their descendants.

Two parties went into the convention.  On one
point, of course, they were agreed, else they would
never have come together at all, — that a united
government under the Articles of Confederation
was a failure, and, unless some remedy should be
speedily devised, States with common local interests would gravitate into separate and perhaps
antagonistic nationalities.  But the differences between these two parties were radical, and for a
time seemed insurmountable.  One proposed simply to repair the Articles of Confederation as they
might overhaul a machine that was out of gear;
the other proposed to form an altogether new Con-

stitution. One wanted a merely federal government; not, however, meaning by that term what the other party — soon, nevertheless, to be known as Federalists — were striving for, but a confederation of States, each independent of all the rest and supreme in its own right, while consenting to unite with the rest in a limited government for the administration of certain common interests.[1]

This idea of the independence of the States was a survival of the old colonial system, when each colony under its distinct relation to the crown had attained a growth of its own with its separate interests. Each of these colonies had become a State. The Revolution had secured to each, it was maintained, a separate independence, achieved, it was true, by united efforts, but not therefore binding them together as a single nation. It was held

---

[1] Those who were zealous for state rights, and opposed to a central government, called the system they wished to reëstablish a Federal System, — a confederacy of States. It was too convenient and probably too popular a term to be lost, and the other party adopted it when the new Constitution was formed. *The Federalist* was the name chosen for the volume in which were collected the papers, written first under the signature of "A Citizen of New York," but afterward changed to "Publius," in support of the new Constitution, by Hamilton, Madison, and Jay. In one of the earlier papers Mr. Hamilton refers to the Articles of Confederation, which were to be superseded, as the Federal Constitution; but in the later papers Madison is careful to refer to the proposed form of government as the Federal Constitution, and Federal soon came to be the distinguishing name of the party which first came into power under the new Constitution. Whatever may be said of Madison's other title, his right to that of father of the Federal party can hardly be disputed.

as a legitimate result of that doctrine that each
State, not the people of the State, whether many
or few, should be represented by the same number of votes in a federal government as they were
under the Articles of Confederation, because such
a government was a union of States, not of a
people.

All men, it was argued, — going back to a state
of nature, — are equally free and independent;
and when a government is formed every man has
an equal share by natural right in its formation
and in its subsequent conduct.    While numbers
are few, every member of the State exercises his
individual right in person, and none can rightfully
do more than this, however wise, or powerful, or
rich he may be.    But when government by the
whole body of the people becomes cumbersome
and inconvenient through increase of numbers,
the individual citizen loses none of his rights by
intrusting their exercise to representatives, in
choosing and instructing whom all have an equal
voice.    So when States are united in a confederacy
each State has the same relation to that government that individuals have to each other in a
single State.    They are free and equal, and none
has a larger share of rights in the confederacy
because its people are more numerous, or because
it is richer or more powerful, than the rest.    In
such a confederacy it is not the individual citizen
who is to be represented, but the individual State.
In such a confederacy there would be the same

representation for a State, say of ten thousand inhabitants, as for one of fifty thousand. This, it was maintained, preserved equality of suffrage in the equality of States ; while the representation of the individual citizens of the States would be in reality inequality of suffrage, because the autonomy of the State would be lost sight of. If in such a case it were asked what had become of the rights which the majority of forty thousand had inherited from nature, the answer was that those rights were preserved and represented in the state government. The difficulty, nevertheless, remained : how to reconcile in practice this doctrine of the equal rights of States, where there might be a minority of persons, with the actual rights of the whole people where, according to the underlying democratic doctrine, the good of the whole must be decided by the larger number.

Those who proposed only to amend the old Articles of Confederation, and opposed a new Constitution, objected that a government formed under such a Constitution would be not a federal but a national government. Luther Martin said, when he returned to Maryland, that the delegates "appeared totally to have forgot the business for which we were sent. . . . We had not been sent to form a government over the inhabitants of America considered as individuals. . . . That the system of government we were intrusted to prepare was a government over these thirteen States, but that in our proceedings we adopted principles which would be right and proper only on the supposition that there were no state governments at all, but that all the inhabitants of this extensive continent were in their individual capacity, without government, and in a state of nature." He added that " in the whole system there was but one federal feature, the appointment of the senators by the States in their sovereign capacity, that is, by their legislatures, and the equality of suffrage in that branch; but it was said that this feature was only federal in appearance."

The Senate, the second house as it was called in the convention, was in part created, it is needless to say, to meet, or rather in obedience to, reasoning like this. There was almost nobody who would have been willing to abandon the state governments, as there was next to nobody who wanted a monarchy. " We were eternally troubled," Martin said, " with arguments and precedents from the British government." He could not get beyond the fixed notion that those whom he opposed were determined to establish " one general government over this extensive continent, of a monarchical nature." If he, and those who agreed with him, sincerely believed this to be true, it was natural enough that the frequent allusions to British precedents, as wise rules for American guidance in constructing a government, should be looked upon as an unmistakable hankering after lost flesh-pots. Should the state governments be swept away, it might be that, in time of danger from without or of peril from internal dissensions, the country, under " a government of a monarchical nature," might drift back to its old allegiance. If those who feared, or said they feared, this were not quite sincere, the temptation was almost irresistible to use such arguments to arouse popular prejudice against political opponents. It is curious that Madison seemed quite unconscious of how much the frequent allusions in his articles in " The Federalist " to the British Constitution might strengthen these accusations of the opposition ; while he half believed that the same thing in others showed in them a leaning toward England, from which he knew that he himself was quite free.

The Luther Martin protestants were too radical to remain in the convention to the end, when they saw that such a confederacy as they wanted was impossible. But there were not many who went the length they did in believing that a strong central government was necessarily the destruction of the state governments. Still fewer were those who would have brought this about if they could. That the rights of the States must be preserved was the general opinion and determination, and it was not difficult to do this by limiting the powers of the higher government, or federal as it soon came to be called, and by the organization of the second house, the Senate, in which all the States had an equal representation. The smaller States were satisfied with this concession, and the larger

were willing to make it, not only for the sake of
the Union, but because of the just estimate in
which they held the rights belonging to all the
States alike. The real difficulty, as Madison said
in the debate on that question, and as he repeated
again and again after that question was settled,
was not between the larger and smaller States,
but between the North and the South ; between
those States that held slaves and those that had
none.

Slavery in the Constitution, which has given so
much trouble to the Abolitionists of this century,
and indeed to everybody else, gave quite as much
in the last century to those who put it there. Many
of the wisest and best men of the time, Southerners
as well as Northerners, and among them Madison,
were opposed to slavery. They could see little
good in it, hardly even any compensation for the
existence of a system so full of evil. There was
hardly a State in the Union at that time that had
not its emancipation society ; and there was hardly
a man of any eminence in the country who was
not an officer, or at least a member, of such a society. Everywhere north of South Carolina, slavery
was looked upon as a misfortune which it was
exceedingly desirable to be free from at the earliest possible moment ; everywhere north of Mason
and Dixon's line, measures had already been taken,
or were certain soon to be taken, to put an end to
it ; and by the ordinance for the government of
all the territory north of the Ohio River it was

absolutely prohibited by Congress in the same year in which the Constitutional Congress met.

But it was, nevertheless, a thing to the continued existence of which the anti-slavery people of that time could consent without any violation of conscience. Bad as it was, unwise, wasteful, cruel, a mockery of every pretense of respect for the rights of man, they did not believe it to be absolutely wicked. If they had so believed, let us hope they would have washed their hands of it. As it was, it was only a question of expediency whether, for the sake of the Union, they should protect the system of slavery, and give to the slaveholders, as slaveholders, a certain degree of political power. To refuse to admit a slaveholding State into the Union did not occur, probably, to the most earnest opponent of the system ; for that would have been simply to say that there should be no Union. That was what Madison meant in saying so repeatedly that the real difficulty in the way was, not the difference between the large and the small States, but the difference between the slaveholding and the non-slaveholding States. If there could be no conciliation on that point there could be no Union.

Some hoped, perhaps, rather than believed, that slavery was likely to disappear ere long at the South as it was disappearing at the North. It is an impeachment of their intelligence, however, to suppose that they relied much upon any such hope. The simple truth is that slavery was then, as it

continued to be for three quarters of a century
longer, the paramount interest of the South. To
withstand or disregard it was not merely difficult,
but was to brave immediate possible dangers and
sufferings, which are never voluntarily encountered except in obedience to the highest sense of
duty; or to meet a necessity, from which there was
no manly way of escape. The sense of absolute
duty was wanting; the necessity, it was hoped,
might be avoided by concessions. It can only be
said for those who made them that they did not
see what fruitful seeds of future trouble they were
sowing in the Constitution.

# CHAPTER VIII

## "THE COMPROMISES"

THE question with the North was, how far could it yield; with the South, how far could it encroach. It turned mainly on representation, — on "the unimportant anomaly," as Mr. George Ticknor Curtis calls it in his "History of the Constitution," "of a representation of men without political rights or social privileges." However much they differed upon the subject in the convention, there was nobody then and there who regarded the question as "unimportant;" nor was there a political event to happen for the coming eighty years that it did not influence and generally govern. There were some who maintained at first that the slave population should not be represented at all. Hamilton proposed in the first days of the convention "that the rights of suffrage in the national legislature ought to be proportioned to the number of free inhabitants." Madison was willing to concede this in one branch of the legislature, provided that in the representation in the other house the slaves were counted as free inhabitants. The constitution of the Senate subsequently disposed of that proposition.

But why should slaves be represented at all? "They are not free agents," said Patterson, a delegate to the convention from New Jersey; they "have no personal liberty, no faculty of acquiring property, but, on the contrary, are themselves property, and, like other property, entirely at the will of the master. Has a man in Virginia a number of votes in proportion to the number of his slaves? And if negroes are not represented in the States to which they belong, why should they be represented in the general government? . . . If a meeting of the people was actually to take place in a slave State, would the slaves vote? They would not. Why, then, should they be represented in a federal government?" There could be but one reply, but that was one which it would not have been wise to make. It was slave property that was to be represented, and this would not be submitted to among slaveholders as against each other, while yet they were a unit in insisting upon it in a union with those who were not slaveholders. Among themselves slavery needed no protection; their safety was in equality. But to their great interest every non-slaveholder was, in the nature of things, an enemy; and prudence required that the power either to vote him down or to buy him up should never be wanting. It was as much a matter of instinct as of deliberation, for love of life is the first law. The truth was covered up in Madison's specious assertion that "every peculiar interest, whether in any class of citizens or any

description of States, ought to be secured as far
as possible." The only "peculiar" interest, however, belonging either to citizens or States, that
was imbedded in the Constitution, was slavery.

So Wilson of Pennsylvania asked: " Are they
[the slaves] admitted as citizens — then why are
they not admitted on an equality with white citizens? Are they admitted as property — then why
is not other property admitted into the computa-
tion?" He was willing, however, to concede that
it was a difficulty to be " overcome by the necessity
of compromise."

Never, probably, in the history of legislation,
was there a more serious question debated. Compromise is ordinarily understood to mean an
adjustment by mutual concessions, where there
are rights on both sides. Here it meant whether
the side which had no shadow of right whatever
to that which it demanded would consent to take
a little less than the whole. It was the kind of
compromise made between the bandit and his
victim when the former decides that he will not
put himself to the trouble of shooting the other,
and will even leave him his shirt. It was not
difficult to understand that horses and cattle could
be justly counted only where property was to be
the basis of representation. Yet the slaves, who
were counted, were, in the eye of the law, either
personal property or real estate, and were no
more represented as citizens than if they also had
gone upon all fours. Their enumeration, never-

theless, was carried, and it so increased the representative power of their masters that inequality of citizenship became the fundamental principle of the government. This, of course, was to form an oligarchy, not a democracy. Practically the government was put in the hands of a class, and there it remained from the moment of the adoption of the Constitution to the rebellion of 1860 ; while that class, including those of so little consequence as to own only a slave or two, in its best estate, probably never exceeded ten per centum of the whole people.

There was, if one may venture to say so, a singular confusion in the minds of the venerable fathers of the republic on this subject. They could not quite get rid of the notion that the slaves, being human, ought to be included in the enumeration of population, notwithstanding that their enumeration as citizens must necessarily disappear in their representation as chattels. Slaves, as slaves, were the wealth of the South, as ships, for example, were the wealth of the North; but, being human, the mind was not shocked at having the slaves reckoned as population in fixing the basis of representation, though in reality they only represented the masters' ownership. But nobody would have been at a loss to see the absurdity of counting three fifths of the Northern ships as population. Even a Webster Whig of sixty-five years later could, perhaps, have understood that that was something more than an " unimportant anomaly." There was no clearer-headed man· in the convention than Gouverneur Morris; yet he said that he was "compelled to declare himself reduced to the dilemma of doing injustice to the Southern States or to human nature, and he must do it to the former." C. C. Pinckney of South Carolina declared that he was "alarmed" at such an avowal as that. Yet had the question been one of counting three fifths of the Northern ships in the enumeration of population, Morris would have discovered no "dilemma," and Pinckney nothing to be "alarmed" at. So palpable an outrage on common sense would have been merely laughed at by both.

In reply to Pinckney, however, Morris grew bolder. "It was high time," he said, "to speak out." He came there "to form a compact for the good of America. He hoped and believed that all would enter into such compact. If they would not, he was ready to join with any States that would. But as the compact was to be voluntary, it is in vain for the Eastern States to insist on what the Southern States will never agree to. It is equally vain for the latter to require what the other States can never admit, and he verily believed the people of Pennsylvania will never agree to a representation of negroes;" of negroes, he meant, counted as human beings, not for their own representation, but, as ships might be counted, for the increased representation of those who held them as property. The next day he "spoke out"

Charles Cotesworth Pinckney

still more plainly. "If negroes," he said, "were
to be viewed as inhabitants, . . . they ought to be
added in their entire number, and not in the proportion of three fifths. If as property, the word
' wealth ' was right," — as the basis, that is, of
representation. The distinction that had been set
up by Madison and others between the Northern
and Southern States he considered as heretical and
groundless. But it was persisted in, and " he saw
that the Southern gentlemen will not be satisfied
unless they see the way open to their gaining a
majority in the public councils. . . . Either this
distinction [between the North and the South] is
fictitious or real ; if fictitious, let it be dismissed,
and let us proceed with due confidence. If it be
real, instead of attempting to blend incompatible
things, let us at once take a friendly leave of each
other."

But could they take " a friendly leave of each
other " ? Should a union be secured on the terms
the South offered ? or should it be declined, as
Morris proposed, if it could not be a union of
equality ? The next day Madison again set forth
the real issue, quietly but unmistakably. " It
seemed now," he said, " to be pretty well understood that the real difference of interests lay, not
between the large and small, but between the
Northern and Southern States. The institution
of slavery and its consequences formed the line of
discrimination." There is sometimes great power,
as he well knew, in firm reiteration. So long as

slavery lasted, the lesson he then inculcated was never forgotten. Thenceforward, as then, "the line of discrimination," in Southern politics, lay with "slavery and its consequences." One side would abate nothing of its demands; there could be no "friendly leave" unless the determination, on the other side, to overcome the desire for union and take the consequences was equally firm. When the question again came up, however, Morris had not lost heart. His talk was the talk of a modern abolitionist: —

"He never would concur in upholding domestic slavery. It was a nefarious institution. It was the curse of Heaven on the States where it prevailed. Compare the free regions of the Middle States, where a rich and noble cultivation marks the prosperity and happiness of the people, with the misery and poverty which overspread the barren wastes of Virginia, Maryland, and the other States having slaves. Travel through the whole continent, and you behold the prospect continually varying with the appearance and disappearance of slavery. . . . Proceed southwardly, and every step you take through the great regions of slavery presents a desert increasing with the increasing proportion of these wretched beings. Upon what principle is it that the slaves shall be computed in the representation? Are they men? Then make them citizens, and let them vote. Are they property? Why then is no other property included? The houses in this city [Philadelphia] are worth more than all the wretched slaves who cover the rice swamps of South Carolina. . . . And what is the proposed compensation to the Northern States for a

sacrifice of every principle of right, of every impulse
of humanity ? They are to bind themselves to march
their militia for the defense of the Southern States, for
their defense against those very slaves of whom they
complain. They must supply vessels and seamen in
case of foreign attack. The legislature will have indefi-
nite power to tax them by excises and duties on imports,
both of which will fall heavier on them than on the
Southern inhabitants ; for the Bohea tea used by a
Northern freeman will pay more tax than the whole
consumption of the miserable slave, which consists of
nothing more than his physical subsistence and the rags
that cover his nakedness. . . . Let it not be said that
direct taxation is to be proportioned to representation.
It is idle to suppose that the general government can
stretch its hand directly into the pockets of the people
scattered over so vast a country. . . . He would sooner
submit himself to a tax for paying for all the negroes
in the United States than saddle posterity with such a
Constitution."

So much of this as was not already fact was
prophecy. Yet not many weeks later this impas-
sioned orator put his name to the Constitution,
though it had grown meanwhile into larger pro-
slavery proportions. There was undoubtedly some
sympathy with him among a few of the members ;
but the general feeling was more truly expressed a
few days later by Rutledge of South Carolina, in
the debate on the continuance of the African slave
trade. " Religion and humanity," he said, " had
nothing to do with this question. Interest alone is
the governing principle with nations. The true

question at present is, whether the Southern States shall or shall not be parties to the Union. If the Northern States consult their interest, they will not oppose the increase of slaves, which will increase the commodities of which they will become the carriers." The response came from Connecticut, Oliver Ellsworth saying: "Let every State import what it pleases. The morality or wisdom of slavery are considerations belonging to the States themselves. What enriches a part enriches the whole," — especially Newport and its adjacent coasts, he might have added, with its trade to the African coast.

But a Virginian, George Mason, had another tone. He called the traffic "infernal." "Slavery," he went on, "discourages arts and manufactures. The poor despise labor when performed by slaves. They prevent the emigration of whites, who really enrich and strengthen a country. They produce the most pernicious effect on manners. Every master of slaves is born a petty tyrant. They bring the judgment of Heaven on a country. As nations cannot be rewarded or punished in the next world, they must be in this. By an inevitable chain of causes and effects, Providence punishes national sins by national calamities."

These were warnings worth heeding. But Ellsworth retorted with a sneer: "As he had never owned a slave, he could not judge of the effect of slavery on character." He said, however, that, "if it was to be considered in a moral light, we ought to go farther, and free those already in the country." But, so far from that, he thought it would be "unjust toward South Carolina and Georgia," in whose "sickly rice swamps" negroes died so fast, should there be any intermeddling to prevent the importation of fresh Africans to labor, and, of course, to perish there. Perhaps it was this shrewd argument of the Connecticut delegate that suggested, half a century afterward, to a Mississippi agricultural society, the economical calculation that it was cheaper to use up a gang of negroes every few years, and supply its place by a fresh gang from Virginia, than rely upon the natural increase that would follow their humane treatment as men and women. His colleague, Roger Sherman, came to Ellsworth's aid. It would be, he thought, the duty of the general government to prohibit the foreign trade in slaves, and, should this be left in its power, it would probably be done. But he would not, if the Southern States made it the condition of consenting to the Constitution that the trade should be protected, leave it in the power of the general government to do that which he acknowledged that it should and probably would do.

Delegates from Georgia and the Carolinas declared that to be the condition, — among them C. C. Pinckney of South Carolina. "He should consider," he said, "a rejection of the clause as an exclusion of South Carolina from the Union." Nevertheless he said to the people at home, when

they came together to consider the Constitution:
" We are so weak that by ourselves we could not
form a union strong enough for the purpose of
effectually protecting each other. Without union
with the other States, South Carolina must soon
fall." On the part of that State it had been a
game of brag all along. The first lesson in the
South Carolinian policy was given in the Constitutional Convention. Of the result, this was
Pinckney's summing up to his constituents : —

" By this settlement we have secured an unlimited importation of negroes for twenty years ; nor is it declared
that the importation shall be then stopped ; it may be
continued. We have a security that the general government can never emancipate them, for no such authority
is granted. . . . We have obtained a right to recover
our slaves, in whatever part of America they may take
refuge, which is a right we had not before. In short,
considering all circumstances, we have made the best
terms, for the security of this species of property, it was
in our power to make. We would have made better if
we could, but on the whole I do not think them bad."

A more moderate and a more significant statement could hardly have been made.

On the foreign slave trade Madison had little
to say, but, like most of the Southern delegates
north of the Carolinas, he was opposed to it.
" Twenty years," he said, " will produce all the
mischief that can be apprehended from the liberty
to import slaves. So long a term will be more
dishonorable to the American character than to

say nothing about it in the Constitution." The words are a little ambiguous, though he is his own reporter. But what he meant evidently was, that any protection of the trade would dishonor the nation; for at another point of the debate, on the same day, he said that "he thought it wrong to admit in the Constitution the idea that there could be property in men." Such property he was anxious to protect as the great Southern interest, so long as it lasted; but he was not willing to strengthen it by permitting the continuance of the African slave trade for twenty years longer under the sanction of the Constitution. But he held it to be, as he wrote in "The Federalist," "a great point gained in favor of humanity that a period of twenty years may terminate forever within these States a traffic which has so long and so loudly upbraided the barbarism of modern policy." He added, "The attempt that had been made to pervert this clause into an objection against the Constitution, by representing it as a criminal toleration of an illicit practice," was a misconstruction which he did not think deserving of an answer.

It was, in fact, a bargain which he had not approved of, and did not now probably care to talk about. It was made at the suggestion of Gouverneur Morris, who moved that the foreign slave trade, a navigation act, and a duty on exports be referred for consideration to a committee. "These things," he said, "may form a bargain among the Northern and Southern States." When the com-

mittee reported in favor of the slave trade, C. C.
Pinckney proposed that its limitation should be
extended from 1800 to 1808. Gorham of Massachusetts seconded the motion, and it was carried
by the addition of the votes of New Hampshire,
Massachusetts, and Connecticut to those of Maryland, North Carolina, South Carolina, and Georgia.

The committee also reported the substitution of
a majority vote for that of two thirds in legislation
relating to commerce. The concession was made
without much difficulty, a Georgia delegate and
three of the four South Carolina delegates favoring
it, two of the latter frankly saying they did so to
gratify New England. It was, C. C. Pinckney
said, "the true interest of the Southern States to
have no regulation of commerce;" but he assented
to this proposition, and his constituents "would be
reconciled to this liberality," because, among other
considerations, of "the liberal conduct [of the New
England States] towards the views of South Carolina." There was no question of the meaning of
this sudden avowal of friendly feeling. Jefferson
relates in his "Ana," on the authority of George
Mason, a member of the convention, that Georgia
and South Carolina had "struck up a bargain with
the three New England States, that if they would
admit slaves for twenty years, the two southernmost
States would join in changing the clause which
required two thirds of the legislature in any vote."

The settlement of these questions was an opportune moment for the introduction of that relating

to fugitive slaves. Butler of South Carolina immediately proposed a section which should secure their return to their masters, and it was passed without a word. As Pinckney said in the passage already quoted, when he went back to report to his constituents, "it is a right to recover our slaves, in whatever part of America they may take refuge, which is a right we had not before."

It is notable how complete and final a settlement of the slavery question "these compromises," as they were called, seemed to be to those who made them. They were meant to be, as Mr. Madison called them, "adjustments of the different interests of different parts of the country," and being once agreed upon they were considered as having the binding force and stability of a contract. The evils of slavery were set forth as an element in the negotiation, but no question of essential morality was raised that brought the system within the category of forbidden wrong. Whatever results might follow would be limited, it' was thought, by the terms of the contract; whereas, in fact, the actual results were not foreseen, and could not be guarded against, except by the refusal to enter into any contract whatever.

On all other questions involving political principles, — the just relations of the federal government and the governments of the States; the relations between the larger and the smaller States; the regulation of the functions of the executive, the legislative, and the judicial departments of

government, — on all these the framers of the
Constitution brought to bear the profoundest wisdom. When one reflects upon the magnitude and
character of the work, Madison's conclusion seems
hardly extravagant, that " adding to these considerations the natural diversity of human opinions on
all new and complicated subjects, it is impossible
to consider the degree of concord which ultimately
prevailed as less than a miracle." There were,
nevertheless, the gravest and most anxious doubts
how far the Constitution would stand the test of
time; yet as a system of government for a nation
of freemen it remains to this day practically un-
changed. But where its architects thought themselves wisest they were weakest. That which they
thought they had settled forever was the one thing
which they did not settle. Of all the "adjustments" of the Constitution, slavery was precisely
that one which was not adjusted.

Madison's responsibility for this result was that
of every other delegate, — no more and no less.
Neither he nor they, whether more or less opposed
to slavery, saw in it a system so subversive of the
rights of man that no just government should tol-
erate it. That was reserved for a later generation,
and even that was slow to learn. To the fathers
it was, at worst, only an unfortunate and unhappy
social condition, which it would be well to be rid
of if this could be done without too much sacrifice;
but otherwise, to be submitted to, like any other
misfortune.

While it did exist, however, Madison believed it should be protected, though not encouraged, as a Southern interest. The question resolved itself into one of expediency, — of union or disunion. What disunion would be, he knew, or thought he knew. Perhaps he was mistaken. Disunion, had it come then, might have been the way to a true union. "We are so weak," said C. C. Pinckney, "that by ourselves we could not form a union strong enough for the purpose of effectually protecting each other. Without union with the other States, South Carolina must soon fall." But he was careful to say this at home, not in Philadelphia. In the convention, Madison wrote a month after it adjourned, "South Carolina and Georgia were inflexible on the point of the slaves." What was to be the union which that inflexibility carried was not foreseen. It was the children's teeth that were to be set on edge.

# CHAPTER IX

MADISON's labors for the Constitution did not cease when the convention adjourned, although he was not at that moment in a hopeful frame of mind in regard to it. Within a week of the adjournment he wrote to Jefferson: "I hazard an opinion that the plan, should it be adopted, will neither effectually answer its national object, nor prevent the local mischiefs which excite disgusts against the state governments."

But this feeling seems to have soon passed away. Perhaps, when he devoted himself to a careful study of what had been done, he saw, in looking at it as a whole, how just and true it was in its fair proportions. He now diligently sought to prove how certainly the Constitution would answer its purpose; how wisely all its parts were adjusted; how successfully the obstacles to a perfect union of the States had been, as he thought, overcome; how carefully the rights of the separate States had been guarded, while the needed general government would be secured. Whether there should be an American nation or not depended, as he had believed for years, upon whether a national Constitution could be agreed upon. Now that it was framed he believed that upon its adoption depended whether there should be, or should not be, a nation. In September, as he wrote to Jefferson, he was in doubt; in February he wrote to Pendleton : " I have for some time been persuaded that the question on which the proposed Constitution must turn is the simple one, whether the Union shall or shall not be continued. There is, in my opinion, no middle ground to be taken."

Those who would have called a second convention to revise the labors of the first had no sympathy from him. He not only doubted if the work could be done so well again ; he doubted if it could be done at all. With him, it was this Constitution or none. " Every man," he said in " The Federalist," referring to a picture he had just drawn of the perils of disunion, — " every man who loves peace, every man who loves his country, every man who loves liberty, ought to have it ever before his eyes, that he may cherish in his heart a due attachment to the Union of America, and be able to set a due value on the means of preserving it." This " means " was the Constitution.

Of the eighty papers of " The Federalist " he wrote twenty-nine ; Hamilton writing forty-six, and Jay only five. These famous essays, of wider repute than any other American book, are yet more generally accepted upon faith than upon knowledge. But at that time, when the new Constitution was in the mind and on the tongue of

every thoughtful man, they were eagerly read as
they followed each other rapidly in the columns of
a New York newspaper.  They were an armory,
wherein all who entered into the controversy could
find such weapons as they could best handle.  What
governments had been, what governments ought to
be, and what the political union of these American
States would be under their new Constitution,
were questions on which the writers of these papers
undertook to answer all reasonable inquiries, and
to silence all cavils.  Madison would undoubtedly
have written more than his two fifths of them, had
he not been called upon early in March to return
to Virginia ; for the work was of the deepest interest to him, and the popularity of the papers would
have stimulated to exertion one as indolent as he
was industrious.

But the canvass for the election of delegates to
the Constitutional Convention of Virginia called
him home.  He had been nominated as the representative of his county, and his friends had urged
him to return before the election, for there was
reason to fear that the majority was on the wrong
side.  Henry, Mason, Randolph, Lee, and others
among the most influential men of Virginia, were
opposed to the Constitution.  There must be somebody in the convention to meet strong men like
these, and Madison was urged to take the stump
and canvass for his own election.  Even this he
was willing to do at this crisis, if need be, though
he said it would be at the sacrifice of every private

inclination, and of the rule which hitherto from the beginning of his public career he had strictly adhered to, — never to ask, directly or indirectly, for votes for himself.

It is quite possible, even quite probable, that Mr. Madison had little of that gift which has always passed for eloquence, and is, indeed, eloquence of a certain kind. If we may trust the reports of his contemporaries, though he wanted some of the graces of oratory, he was not wanting in the power of winning and convincing. His arguments were often, if not always, prepared with care. If there was no play of fancy, there was no forgetfulness of facts. If there was lack of imagination, there was none of historical illustration, when the subject admitted it. If manner was forgotten, method was not. His aim was to prove and to hold fast ; to make the wrong clear, and to put the right in its place ; to appeal to reason, not to passion, nor to prejudice ; to try his cause by the light of clear logic, hard facts, and sound learning ; to convince his hearers of the truth, as he believed in it, not to take their judgment captive by surprise with harmonious modulation and grace of movement. Not his neighbors only, but the most zealous of the Federalists of the State, sent him to the convention. It was there that such eloquence as he possessed was peculiarly needed. The ground was to be fought over inch by inch, and with antagonists whom it would be difficult, if not impossible, to beat. There was to be contest over

every word of the Constitution from its first to its
last. "Give me leave," cried Patrick Henry in
his opening speech, "to demand what right had
they to say 'We the people' instead of 'We the
States'?" He began at the beginning. It was
the gage of the coming battle; the defenders were
challenged to show that any better union than that
already in existence was needed, and that in this
new Constitution a better union was furnished.

As month after month passed away while the
Constitution was before the people for adoption,
the anxiety of the Federalists grew, lest the requisite nine States should not give their assent. But
when eight were secured there was room to hope
even for unanimity, if Virginia should come in as
the ninth. Should she say Yes, the Union might
be perfect; for the remaining States would be
almost sure to follow her lead. But should she
say No, the final result would be doubtful, even if
the requisite nine should be secured by the acquiescence of one of the smaller States. This answer
could not, of course, depend altogether upon one
man, but it did depend more upon Madison than
upon anybody else.

The convention was in session nearly a month.
At the end of a fortnight he was not hopeful.
"The business," he wrote to Washington, "is in
the most ticklish state that can be imagined. The
majority will certainly be very small, on whatever
side it may finally lie; and I dare not encourage
much expectation that it will be on the favorable

side." But his fears stimulated rather than discouraged him. He was always on his feet; always ready to meet argument with argument; always prompt to appeal from passion to reason; quick to brush aside mere declamation, and to bring the minds of his hearers back to a calm consideration of how much was at stake, and of the weight of the responsibility resting on that convention. Others were no less earnest and diligent than he ; but he was easily chief, and the burden and heat of the day fell mainly upon him. Probably when the convention assembled the majority were opposed to the Constitution ; but its adoption was carried at last by a vote of eighty-nine to seventy-nine. Thenceforth opposition in the remaining States was hopeless.

New Hampshire — though the fact was not known in Virginia — preceded that State by a few days in accepting the Constitution, so that the requisite nine were secured before the convention at Richmond came to a decision. But it was her decision, nevertheless, that really settled, so far as can be seen now, the question of a permanent Union. Had the vote of Virginia been the other way it is not likely that Hamilton would have carried New York, or that North Carolina and Rhode Island would have finally decided not to be left in solitude outside. What the history of the nine united States only, with four disunited States among them, might have been, it is impossible to know, and quite useless to conjecture. The

conditions which some of the States attached to the
act of adoption, the addition of a Bill of Rights,
proposed amendments to the Constitution, and the
suggestion of submitting it to a second convention, were matters of comparatively little moment,
when the majority of ten delegates was secured at
Richmond.    These were questions that could be
postponed.    " The delay of a few years," Madison
wrote to Jefferson, " will assuage the jealousies
which have been artificially created by designing
men, and will at the same time point out the faults
which call for amendment."

Immediately after the adjournment of the Richmond Convention he returned to New York, where
the confederate Congress was still in session.
That body had little to do now but decide upon
the time and place of the inauguration of the new
government.    Madison had entered upon his thirty-
eighth year, and we get an interesting glimpse of
him as he appeared at this time of his life to an
intelligent foreigner.    " Mr. Warville Brissot has
just arrived here," he wrote to Jefferson in August,
1788.    This was Brissot de Warville, a Frenchman
of the new philosophy, — whose head, nevertheless,
his compatriots cut off a few years later, — then
traveling in America to observe the condition and
progress of the new republic.    His tour extended
to nearly all the States ; he met with most of the
distinguished men of the country ; and he made a
careful and intelligent use of his many opportunities for observation.    On his return to France he

wrote an entertaining volume, — " New Travels in the United States of America," — still to be found in some old libraries.  What he says of Madison is worth repeating, not only for the impression he made upon an observant stranger, but as the evidence of the contemporary estimate of his character and reputation, which De Warville must have gathered from others.

" The name of Madison," he writes, " celebrated in America, is well known in Europe by the merited eulogium made of him by his countryman and friend, Mr. Jefferson.

" Though still young, he has rendered the greatest services to Virginia, to the American Confederation, and to liberty and humanity in general.  He contributed much, with Mr. White, in reforming the civil and criminal codes of his country.  He distinguished himself particularly in the convention for the acceptation of the new federal system.  Virginia balanced a long time in adhering to it.  Mr. Madison determined to it the members of the convention by his eloquence and logic.  This republican appears to be about thirty-eight years of age.  He had, when I saw him, an air of fatigue ; perhaps it was the effect of the immense labors to which he has devoted himself for some time past.  His look announces a censor, his conversation discovers the man of learning, and his reserve was that of a man conscious of his talents and of his duties.

" During the dinner, to which he invited me, they spoke of the refusal of North Carolina to accede to the new Constitution.  The majority against it was one hundred.  Mr. Madison believed that this refusal would have no weight on the minds of the Americans, and that it would not impede the operations of Congress. I told him that though this refusal might be regarded as a trifle in America, it would have great weight in Europe; that they would never inquire there into the motives which dictated it, nor consider the small consequence of this State in the confederation; that it would be regarded as a germ of division, calculated to retard the operations of Congress; and that certainly this idea would prevent the resurrection of American credit.

" Mr. Madison attributed this refusal to the attachment of a great part of the inhabitants of that State to their paper money and their tender act. He was much inclined to believe that this disposition would not remain a long time."

In October the Virginia Assembly met. Two thirds of its members were opposed to the new Constitution, and at their head was Patrick Henry, his zeal against it not in the least abated because he had been defeated in the late convention. The acceptance of the Constitution by that representative body could not be recalled. But the Assembly could, at least, protest against it, and was led by Henry to call upon Congress to convene a second national convention to do over again the work of the first. The legislature was to elect senators for the first Senate under the new government; and it was also to divide the State into districts for its representation in the lower house of Congress. In ordinary fairness, as the State had, in a popular convention, so recently accepted the Constitution, the party then in the majority was entitled to at least one of the representatives in the Senate. But Henry nominated both, and could command votes enough to elect them. In modern party usage this would seem quite unobjectionable ; indeed, a modern politician who should not use such an advantage for his party would be considered as unfit for practical politics. But a hundred years ago it was thought sharp practice, and a fair proportion of Henry's partisans refused to be bound by it. One of Henry's nominees was elected by a majority of twenty over Madison ; but in the case of the other that majority was reduced more than half, and a change of five more votes would have elected Madison.

He had, however, neither expected nor wished to be sent to the Senate, while he did hope to be elected to the House of Representatives. The Senate was intended to be the more dignified body, requiring in its members a certain style of living for which wealth was indispensable. Madison had not the means to give that kind of social support to official position ; but he could afford to belong to that body where a member was not the less respectable because his whole domestic establishment might be a bachelor's room in a boarding-house.

Virginia was, as he wrote to Washington, " the only instance among the ratifying States in which the politics of the legislature are at variance with the sense of the people, expressed by their representatives in convention." This had enabled Henry and a majority of his friends to elect senators who, representing "the politics of the legislature," did not represent "the sense of the people" in regard to the national Constitution. But in the election of members of the House of Representatives, the sense of the people was to be again appealed to, and a new way must be devised for asserting the supremacy of legislative power. The cleverness of Elbridge Gerry of Massachusetts, many years later, under similar circumstances, introduced a new word into the language of the country, and, it was supposed at the time, a new device in American politics. But what has since been known as "Gerrymandering" was really the invention of Patrick Henry. This method of arranging counties into congressional districts in accordance with their political affinities, without regard to their geographical lines, Henry attempted to do with Mr. Madison's own county. By joining it to distant counties it was expected that an anti-Federal majority would be secured large enough to insure his defeat. The attempt to elect him to the Senate was, Madison wrote to Jefferson, "defeated by Mr. Henry, who is omnipotent in the present legislature." He adds that Henry " has taken equal pains, in forming the counties into districts for the election of representatives, to associate with Orange such as are most devoted to his politics, and most likely to be swayed by the prejudices excited against me." The scheme, however, was unsuccessful, perhaps partly because of the indig-

nation which so dishonorable a measure to defeat
a political opponent excited throughout the State.
Madison entered upon an active canvass of his
district against James Monroe, who had been
nominated as a moderate anti-Federalist, and defeated him.   It was winter time, and in the exposure of some of his long rides his ears were
frozen.   In later life he sometimes laughingly
pointed to the scars of these wounds received, he
said, in the service of his country.

Thus Henry's " Gerrymander," like many another useful and curious device, brought neither
profit nor credit to the original inventor.   Had
Henry acted in the broader spirit of the modern
politician, who sees that he serves himself best
who serves his party best, he would have disposed
of every Federal county in the State as he disposed of Orange.   As it was, he only aroused a
good deal of indignation and defeated himself by
openly aiming to gratify his personal resentments.
Had he scattered his shot for the general good of
the party, he would, perhaps, have brought down
his particular bird.

# CHAPTER X

## THE FIRST CONGRESS

THE confederate Congress, at its final session in 1788, had fixed the time for the election of President and Vice-President under the Constitution, and the time and place for the meeting of the first Congress of the new government. The day appointed was the first Wednesday of the following March, and, as that date fell on the fourth of the month, a precedent was established which has ever since been observed in the installation of a new President. The place was not so easily determined. The choice lay between New York and Philadelphia, and the struggle was prolonged, not because the question of the temporary seat of government was of much moment, but because of the influence the decision might have upon the future settlement of the permanent place for the capital.

No quorum of the new Congress was present at New York on March 4, 1789, and neither house was organized until early in April. On the 23d Washington arrived; and on the 30th he took the oath of office as first President of the United States, standing on the balcony of Federal Hall, at the corner of Wall and Broad streets, a site now occupied by another building used as the sub-treasury. A week before, when the ceremonies proper for such an occasion were a subject of discussion in Congress, the question of fitting titles for the President and Vice-President came up for consideration. It was decided that when the President arrived the Vice-President should meet him at the door of the senate chamber, lead him to the chair, and then, in a formal address, inform him that the two houses were ready to witness the administration of the oath of office. "Upon this," says John Adams in a letter written three years afterward, "I arose in my place and asked the advice of the Senate, in what form I should address him, whether I should say 'Mr. Washington,' 'Mr. President,' 'Sir,' 'May it please your Excellency,' or what else? I observed that it had been common while he commanded the army to call him 'His Excellency,' but I was free to own it would appear to me better to give him no title but 'Sir,' or 'Mr. President,' than to put him on a level with a governor of Bermuda, or one of his own ambassadors, or a governor of any one of our States."

Thereupon the question went to a conference committee of both houses, who reported that no other title would be proper for either President or Vice-President, at any time, than those which were given by the Constitution. To this report the Senate disagreed and appointed a new committee.

This proposed that the President should be called " His Highness the President of the United States and Protector of their Liberties." When wise men are absurd they presume on their prerogative. The Senate accepted the report, but the House had the good sense to reject it, consenting, however, to leave the question in abeyance. On these proceedings Mr. Madison thus commented in a letter to Jefferson : —

" My last inclosed copies of the President's inaugural speech, and the answer of the House of Representatives. I now add the answer of the Senate. It will not have escaped you that the former was addressed with a truly republican simplicity to George Washington, President of the United States. The latter follows the example, with the omission of the personal name, but without any other than the constitutional title. The proceeding on this point was, in the House of Representatives, spontaneous. The imitation by the Senate was extorted. The question became a serious one between the two houses. J. Adams espoused the cause of titles with great earnestness. His friend, R. H. Lee, although elected as a republican enemy to an aristocratic Constitution, was a most zealous second. The projected title was, His Highness the President of the United States and the Protector of their Liberties. Had the project succeeded, it would have subjected the President to a severe dilemma, and given a deep wound to our infant government."

Washington has sometimes been accused of wishing for the title of " His Highness," and of having

suggested it. Had this been true, Madison would
have been certain to know it, and he was quite
incapable of asserting in that case that such a
title would have been to the President "a severe
dilemma." About Mr. Adams he was perhaps
mistaken, as he might easily have been, since he
was not a member of the Senate, and probably
heard only a confused report of how the question
was brought before that body. As Mr. Adams's
letter, quoted just now, shows, he regarded the
charge as a calumny and resented it. He gave
them, according to his own statement, no other
opinion than that he preferred "Sir," or "Mr.
President," as a more proper address than "Excellency," a title then, as now, pertaining to governors
of States. He probably took no further part in
the debate, but it is not impossible that he may in
private have avowed a preference for some other
and higher title than either "Mr. President" or
"Your Excellency." "For," he said in the explan-
atory letter to his friend, "I freely own that I
think decent and moderate titles, as distinctions
of offices, are not only harmless, but useful in
society; and that in this country, where I know
them to be prized by the people as well as their
magistrates as highly as by any people or any
magistrates in the world, I should think some distinction between the magistrates of the national
government and those of the state governments
proper." A distinction might be proper enough if
there were to be any titles whatever; but certainly

they were the wiser who preferred good homespun to threadbare old clothes. Had rags of that sort been made a legal uniform, it is almost appalling to reflect upon the absurdities to which the national fondness for titles would have carried us.

From March 4 to April 1, though the House of Representatives met daily, there were not members enough present to make a quorum. The first real business brought before the House, except that relating to its organization, was introduced by Madison, two days after the inauguration. It was a proposition to raise a revenue by duties on imports, and by a tonnage duty on all vessels, American and foreign, bringing goods, wares, or merchandise into the United States. The essential weakness of the late Confederacy was, first of all, to be remedied by uniform rules for the regulation of trade. Revenue must be provided for the support of government, and that in a way which should not be oppressive to the people. Commerce, Mr. Madison said, "ought to be as free as the policy of nations will admit," but government must be supported, and taxes the least burdensome and most easily collected are those derived from duties on imports. He agreed, however, as he said on the second day of the debate, with those who would so adjust the duties on foreign goods as to protect the "infant manufactories" of the country. With little interruption this subject was debated for the first six weeks of the opening session of the First Congress. No other could have been hit upon to test so thoroughly the strength of the new bond of union. It was to brush aside all those trade regulations in the several States which each had hitherto thought essential to its prosperity. Every interest in the country was to be considered, and their different, sometimes opposing, claims to be reconciled.

New England was sure that, should the tax on molasses be too high, the distilleries would be shut up, and a great New England industry destroyed. Nor would the injury stop there. The fisheries, as well as the distilleries, would be ruined. For three fifths of the fish put up for the West Indies could find no market anywhere else ; and a market existed there only because molasses was taken in exchange. A prohibitory duty on that article, or a duty that should seriously interfere with its importation, would wellnigh destroy the fisheries. What then would become of the nursery of American seamen ? With no seamen there would be no shipbuilding. What sadder picture than this of a New England without rum, without codfish, without seamen, and without ships ! One can easily conceive that even in that restrained and dignified First Congress there was no want of serious and alarmed expostulation, and even some threatening talk from such men as the tranquil Goodhue, the thoughtful and scholarly Ames, and the impulsive Gerry.

Then the South, for her part, was alarmed lest, among other things, too high a tonnage duty should

leave her tobacco, her rice and indigo, rotting in
the fields and warehouses for want of ships to take
them to market.   She had no ships of her own and
could have none, and she invited the ships of the
rest of the world to come for her products and
bring in return all she needed for her own consumption.   The picture of the possible ruin of New
England was as nothing to that of the Southern
planter scanning the horizon with weary eyes in
vain for the sight of a sail, while behind him
was a dangerous crowd of hungry blacks with
nothing to do.   That desolation seemed complete
to the southernmost States when it was also proposed to levy a tax of ten dollars upon every slave
imported.   In short, the whole subject bristled
with difficulties.   The problem was nothing more
nor less than how to tax everything, and at the
same time convince everybody that the scheme
was for the general good, while nobody's special
interests were sacrificed.   The "infant indus-
tries," to which Mr. Madison alluded, really received no special consideration in the final adjustment, and they were too feeble then even to cry for
nursing.   They have grown stronger since, though
they are "infants" still; and they should never
cease to be grateful to him who, however unwittingly, gave them a name to live by for a hundred
years.

But the most remarkable part of the debate was
that upon the proposition of Mr. Parker of Virginia to impose a duty upon the importation of

slaves. Could the progress of events have been foreseen, that proposal might have been regarded as meant to protect an "infant industry" of the northernmost slave States. But the wildest imagination then could not conceive of the domestic slave trade of a few years later, when a chief source of the prosperity of Virginia would be her perennial crop of young men and women to be shipped for New Orleans and a market. But Mr. Parker had no ulterior motive when he avowed his regret that the Constitution had failed to prohibit the importation of slaves from Africa, and hoped that the duty he proposed would prevent, in some degree, a traffic which he pronounced "irrational and inhuman." It would have been difficult to have found a Virginian of that day who would not have taken down his shotgun on hearing that there were miscreants prowling about his kitchen doors in the hope of buying up the strongest young people of his household for export to the Southwest.

Judging from the imperfect report of the debate upon the subject, it would seem that the bargain relative to the slave trade, made in the Constitutional Convention of two years before between New England and the two southernmost States, might still hold good. Or there may have been a new bargain; or, perhaps, both sides trusted to a tacit recognition of the eternal fitness of things, and made common cause where legislation threatened at the same time the distillery and the

slave-ship.[1]   At any rate, the extreme Southerners
expressed surprise at the audacity which would
disturb a compromise of the Constitution; the extreme Northerners deprecated it as quite uncalled
for in any consideration of the subject of revenue.
The principle of Mr. Parker's motion, Mr. Sherman of Connecticut thought, was to correct a moral
evil; the principle of the bill before the House was
to raise a revenue.   At some other time he would
be willing to consider the question of taxing the
importation of negroes on the ground of humanity
and policy; but it was a sufficient reason with
him for not admitting it as an object of revenue
that the burden would fall upon two States only.
Fisher Ames of Massachusetts could only take
counsel of his conscience.   From his soul, he said,

[1] Eleven years afterward, when the question of prohibiting the
carrying on the slave trade from American ports came up, one
John Brown of Rhode Island said in Congress, " Our distilleries
and manufactories were all lying idle for want of an extended
commerce.   He had been well informed that on those coasts
[African] New England rum was much preferred to the best
Jamaica spirits, and would fetch a better price.   Why should it
not be sent there, and a profitable return be made ?   Why should
a heavy fine and imprisonment [of slave traders] be made the
penalty for carrying on a trade so advantageous ? "   Sixty years
later still, there was another Brown in Providence, Rhode Island,
who was a member of the Committee of the Kansas Aid Society
of New England.   He was about to withdraw from it for want of
time to attend to its duties, — had, indeed, actually sent in his
resignation, — when news came of the doings of another John
Brown at Harper's Ferry.   The resignation was instantly recalled,
with the remark that it was not a time for Browns to seem to be
backward on the question of slavery.   Such is the irony of coincidence in names.

he detested slavery; and — forgetting, apparently,
that this tax was provided for by the Constitution
— he doubted whether imposing it "would not
have the appearance of authorizing the practice"
of trading in slaves. This was his reason for wishing to postpone the subject. But Mr. Livermore
of New Hampshire was more ingenious still. If
the imported negroes were goods, wares, or merchandise, they would come within the title of the
bill, and be taxed under the general rule of five
per centum, which would be about the same rate
as ten dollars a head; but if they were not goods,
wares, or merchandise, then such importation could
not properly be included in the consideration of
the question of a revenue from duties on such
articles of trade.

Mr. Madison came to the help of his colleague,
and brushed aside the sophistries of the New
England allies of the slave traders. If there were
anything wanting in the title of the bill to cover
this particular duty, it was easy to add it. If the
question was not one of taxation because it was
one of humanity, it would be quite as difficult to
deal with it under any other bill for levying a
duty as under this. If the tax seemed unjust because it bore heavily upon a single class, that
would be a good reason for remitting many taxes
which there was no hesitation in imposing. If ten
dollars seemed a heavy duty, a little calculation
would show that it was only about the proposed
*ad valorem* duty of five per centum on most other

importations. "It is to be hoped," he added, "that by expressing a national disapprobation of this trade we may destroy it, and save ourselves from reproaches, and our posterity the imbecility ever attendant on a country filled with slaves." "If there is any one point," he continued, "in which it is clearly the policy of this nation, so far as we constitutionally can, to vary the practice obtaining under some of the state governments, it is this. . . . It is as much the interest of Georgia and South Carolina as of any in the Union. Every addition they receive to their number of slaves tends to weaken and render them less capable of self-defense. . . . It is a necessary duty of the general government to protect every part of the empire against danger, as well internal as external. Everything, therefore, which tends to increase this danger, though it may be a local affair, yet, if it involves national expense or safety, becomes of concern to every part of the Union, and is a proper subject for the consideration of those charged with the general administration of the government." No Northern man, except Elbridge Gerry of Massachusetts, supported this measure; and none from the Southern States, except three of the Virginia members, with Madison leading. As the foreign slave trade was protected in the Constitution for twenty years by a bargain between the two southernmost States and New England, so now the same influence staved off the imposition of the tax which was a part of the consideration to be given for that constitutional protection of the trade. It is not a creditable fact ; but it is, nevertheless, a fact and a representative one in the history of the United States. And it is to Madison's great honor that he had neither part nor lot in it.

After six weeks of earnest debate, an amicable and satisfactory agreement was made to impose a moderate duty upon pretty much everything imported, except slaves from Africa. It was literally a tariff for revenue ; but it was a settlement that settled nothing definitely, except that the provision of the Constitution for a tax of ten dollars on imported slaves should be a dead letter. Thenceforth the policy of free trade was established, so far as African slaves were concerned, till the traffic was supposed to cease by constitutional limitation and Act of Congress in 1808.[1]

[1] The subsequent legislation on this subject is a curious exemplification of the ingenuity with which any law obnoxious to the owners of slaves was got rid of, when it was clear that it could not be defeated by force of numbers. In 1806 a final attempt was made to impose the duty of ten dollars upon slaves imported, and a resolution passed in favor of it. This was referred to a committee, with instructions to bring in a bill. A bill was reported and pushed so far as a third reading, when it was recommitted, which put it off for a year. When it next appeared it was a bill for the prohibition of the importation of slaves, in accordance with the constitutional provision that the traffic should cease in 1808. The new question, after some debate, in which there was no allusion to the tax, was postponed for further consideration. But it never again came before the House. A month later, February 13, 1807, a bill from the Senate, providing that the foreign slave trade should cease on the first day of the following January, was received and immediately concurred in, and that seems to have

The determination to protect the commercial interests of the country, beyond the point of mere revenue, was more manifest in fixing the rate of duty upon tonnage than in duties upon importations. It was generally agreed, after much debate, that American commerce had better be in American hands, and a difference of twenty cents a ton was made between the tax upon domestic and that upon foreign ships, as a measure of protection to American shipping. Mr. Madison proposed to make it still larger, but the House would only agree to increase it to forty cents on ships belonging to powers with which the United States had no treaties. The Senate, however, refused to admit this distinction, and insisted that all foreign ships should be subject to the same tonnage duty without regard to existing treaties. The House assented, lest the bill should be lost altogether. This proposed differential duty on foreign vessels was as clearly aimed at Great Britain as if that power had been named in the bill. Nor, indeed, was there any attempt at concealment; for it was openly avowed that America had no formidable rival except the English, who already largely controlled the commerce of the United States. In the debates and in the final decision of the question

been silently accepted as disposing of the whole subject. No tax was ever paid; but the importation of slaves, notwithstanding the law to put an end to importation in 1808, continued at the rate, it was estimated, of about fifteen thousand a year. Probably it never ceased altogether till the beginning of the rebellion of 1860.

is shown clearly enough the difference of opinion
and of feeling, which soon made the dividing line
between the two great parties of the first quarter
of a century under the Constitution. Nobody then
foresaw how bitter that difference of party was
to be, nor what disastrous consequences would follow it.

Mr. Madison was among the most zealous of
those who insisted upon a discrimination against
Great Britain. He thought it should be made
for the dignity no less than for the interest of the
United States. He had no fear, he said, " of entering into a commercial warfare with that nation."
England, he believed, could do this country no
harm by any peaceful reprisals she could devise.
She supplied the United States with no article
either of necessity or of luxury that the people of
the United States could not manufacture for themselves. He called those " Anglicists " who did not
agree with him, and who believed that it was in
the power of Great Britain to hinder or to help
immensely the prosperity of the United States. It
was not of so much moment what America bought
of England as it was that England should consent to free trade with her colonies; and on every
account it was wiser to conciliate than to defy Great
Britain ; wiser to induce her to enter into a friendly
commercial alliance than to provoke her to retaliate upon the feeble commerce of this country, upon
which she had so strong a grip. Madison had
shown himself, before this time, half credulous of

the charges of a leaning toward England, and
toward monarchy, made by those who wanted a
congress of petty states against those who wanted
a strong national government.  If, however, there
were Anglicism on one side, so there was quite as
much Gallicism, if not a good deal more, on the
other.  In writing to Jefferson of the probability
that the Senate would make no discrimination in
the tonnage duties, he said that in that case " Great
Britain will be quieted in the enjoyment of our
trade as she may please to regulate it, and France
discouraged from her efforts at a competition which
it is not less our interest than hers to promote."
Whatever may be thought of this first concession
of the new government to England, it is quite as
much the coming party leader as the statesman
who speaks here.  It may not be doubted that he
sincerely thought it to be, as he said, "impolitic,
in every view that can be taken of the subject, to
put Great Britain at once on the footing of the
most favored nation."  But the relation of American interests to English interests was evidently
already associated in his mind with the relations
of France and England, so soon to be the absorb-
ing question in American politics.

The impost act was followed by others hardly
less important in putting the new Constitution into
operation under its first Congress.  The direction
of business seems, by common consent, to have
been intrusted to Mr. Madison among the many
able men of that body ; doubtless because of his

thorough familiarity with the Constitution, and of his methodical ways. He was sure to bring things forward in their due order, to provide judiciously for the more immediate needs. The impost bill secured the means to work with ; the next necessity was to organize the machinery to do the work. Resolutions to create the executive departments of Foreign Affairs, of the Treasury, and of War were offered by Mr. Madison. These were required in general terms by the Constitution, with a single officer at the head of each, to be appointed by the President " by and with the advice and consent of the Senate." The manner of the appointment of subordinate officers was provided for by the Constitution, but the manner of their removal from office was not. Was the tenure of office to be good behavior ? Were the incumbents removable, with or without cause ? If the power of removal existed, did it vest in the power that appointed, that is, in the President and Senate conjointly, or in the President alone ?

As the Constitution was silent, the question had to be settled on its own merits. With all the arguments that could be urged, either on one side or the other, we are familiar enough in our time, coming up as the question so often does in changes in state constitutions and municipal charters, and in the discussion of the necessity for civil service reform. There is this essential difference, however, between now and then : we know the mischiefs that come from the power of official

removal, which were then only dimly apprehended.
The power of removal from office belonged, Mr.
Madison believed, rightfully to the chief magistrate, and, if by some unhappy chance the wrong
man should find his way to that position and abuse
the power intrusted to him, "the wanton removal
of meritorious officers would," he said, "subject
the President to impeachment and removal from
his own high trust."

Lofty political principles like these may still be
found in the platforms of modern political parties, —

"The souls of them fumed-forth, the hearts of them torn-out."

But Mr. Madison believed, at least, that he believed in them.   There is in politics as in religion
an accepted doctrine of justification by faith; and
this, perhaps, sustained him when, twelve years
later, as Jefferson's secretary of state, he learned
from his chief that, as "Federalists seldom died
and never resigned," party necessities must find a
way of supplementing the law of nature.   Jefferson was a little timid in applying the remedy, but
Madison lived long enough to see Jackson boldly
remove, in the course of his administration, about
two thousand office-holders, whose places he wanted
as rewards for his own political followers.   From
that time to this, there has not been a President
who might not, if Madison's doctrine was sound,
have been impeached for a "wanton" abuse of
power.

Though the Constitution had been adopted by the States, it was not without objections by some of them. To meet these objections Mr. Madison proposed twelve amendments declaratory of certain fundamental popular rights, which, it was thought by many persons, were not sufficiently guarded by the original articles. This, also, was left to him to do, no doubt because of his thorough knowledge of the Constitution and of the points wherein it was still imperfect, as well as those wherein it had better not be meddled with. The amendments, as finally agreed to after long debate, were essentially those which he proposed, and in due time ten of them were ratified by the States. The two that were not accepted referred only to the number of representatives in the House, and to the pay of members of Congress.

It was hoped that the selection of a place for the permanent seat of government would be made by this Congress. There was much talk of the centres of wealth, of territory, and of population then, and of where such centres might be in the future. But the question was really a sectional one. The Northern members were accused of having made a bargain out of doors with the members of the Middle States. The bargain, however, was only this : that, inasmuch as it was hopeless that the actual centre should be chosen as the site for a capital city, a place as near as possible to it should be insisted upon. The South, on the other hand, determined that the seat of government should

be within the boundaries of the Southern States.
That was a foregone conclusion with them, that
needed no bargain.  The nearest navigable river
to the centre of population was the Delaware; but
the jealousy of New York stood in the way of any
selection that favored Philadelphia.  The Susquehanna was proposed.  It empties into Chesapeake Bay.  North of it was, as Mr. Sherman
showed, a population of 1,400,000; and south of it,
1,200,000.  The South wanted the capital on the
Potomac, not because it was the centre of population then, but because it might be at some future
time, from the growth of the West.  On the other
hand, it was insisted that the population south of
the Potomac was then only 960,000, while north
of it there were 1,680,000 people, and that it was
no more accessible from the West than the Susquehanna was.  To many members, moreover, this talk
of the great future of the West seemed hardly
worthy of consideration.  It was " an unmeasur-
able wilderness," and " when it would be settled
was past calculation," Fisher Ames said.  " It
was," he added, " perfectly romantic to make this
decision depend upon that circumstance.  Probably it will be near a century before these people
will be considerable."  He was nearer right when
he said in the same speech " that trade and manufactures will accumulate people in the Eastern
States in proportion of five to three, compared
with the Southern.  The disproportion will, doubtless, continue to be much greater than I have

calculated. It is actually greater at present, for the climate and negro slavery are acknowledged to be unfavorable to population, so that husbandry as well as commerce and manufactures will give more people in the Eastern than in the Southern States." It was, however, finally resolved by the House "that the permanent seat of the government of the United States ought to be at some convenient place on the banks of the river Susquehanna in the State of Pennsylvania;" and a bill accordingly was sent to the Senate.

Had the Senate agreed to this bill, there are some luminous pages of American history that would never have been written; for the progress of events would have taken quite another direction had the influences surrounding the national capital for the first half of this century been Northern instead of Southern. But the Senate did not agree. For "the convenient place on the banks of the Susquehanna" it substituted ten miles square on the river Delaware, beginning one mile from Philadelphia and including the village of Germantown. To this amendment the House agreed, and there, but for Madison, the matter would have ended. He had labored earnestly for the site on the Potomac; but failing in that, he hoped to postpone the question till the next session of Congress, when the representatives from North Carolina would be present. He moved a proviso that the laws of Pennsylvania should remain in force within the district ceded by the State till Congress should

otherwise provide by law. It seems to have been
accepted without consideration, a single member
only saying that he saw no necessity for it. At
any rate, whether that was Mr. Madison's motive
or not, time was gained, for it compelled the return
of the bill to the Senate. This was on September
28, and the next day the session was closed by
adjournment till the following January.

When in that next session the bill came back
from the Senate to the House, a member from
South Carolina said, in the course of debate, that
"a Quaker State was a bad neighborhood for the
South Carolinians." The Senate had also come
to that conclusion, for the bill now proposed that
the capital should be at Philadelphia for ten years
only, and should then be removed to the banks of
the Potomac. It was done, Madison wrote to
Monroe, by a single vote, for two Southern senators voted against it. But the two senators from
North Carolina were now present, and the majority
of one was made sure of somehow.

So much was gained by gaining time, and Madison thought the passage of the bill through the
House was possible, "but attended with great
difficulties." Did he know how these difficulties
were to be overcome? "If the Potomac succeeds,"
he adds, "it will have resulted from a fortuitous
coincidence of circumstances which might never
happen again." What the "fortuitous coincidence" was he does not explain; but the term was
a felicitous euphuism to cover up what in the

blunter political language of our time is called "log-rolling."

The reader of this series of biographies is already familiar with Hamilton's skillful barter of votes for the Potomac site of the capital in exchange for votes in favor of his scheme for the assumption of the state debts. Madison seems not to have been ignorant of the progress of that bargain, with which Jefferson was afterward so anxious to prove that he had nothing to do. Madison earnestly opposed the assumption of the state debts from first to last; but, when he saw that the measure was sure to pass the House, he wrote to Monroe: " I cannot deny that the crisis demands a spirit of accommodation to a certain extent. If the measure should be adopted, I shall wish it to be considered as an unavoidable evil, and *possibly* not the worst side of the dilemma." In other words, he was willing to assent silently to what he believed to be a great injustice to several of the States, provided that the bargain should be a gain to his own State. If Hamilton and Jefferson were sinners in this business, Madison will hardly pass for a saint.

# CHAPTER XI

HAMILTON'S famous report to the First Congress, as secretary of the treasury, was made at the second session in January, 1790. Near the close of the previous session a petition asking for some settlement of the public debt was received and referred to a committee of which Madison was chairman. The committee reported in favor of the petition, and the House accordingly called upon the secretary to prepare a plan " for the support of the public credit."

So far as Hamilton's funding scheme provided for that portion of the debt due to foreigners, it was accepted without demur. There could be no doubt that there the ostensible creditor was the real creditor, who should be paid in full. The report assumed that this was equally true of the domestic debt. A citizen holding a certificate of the indebtedness of the government, no matter how he came by it, nor at what price, was entitled to payment at its face value. But here the question was raised, Was this ostensible creditor the sole creditor? Was he, whose necessities had compelled him to part with the government's note of hand at a large dis-

count when full payment was impossible, to receive
nothing now when at last government was able to
pay in full?  Was it equity to let all the loss fall
upon the original creditor, and all the gain go to
him who had lost nothing originally, and had only
assumed at small cost the risk of a profitable speculation?  Moreover it was charged, and not denied,
that in some of these speculations there had been
no risk whatever; and that, so soon as the tenor
of the report was known, fast-sailing vessels were
dispatched from New York to the Carolinas and
Georgia to buy up public securities held by persons
ignorant of their recent rapid rise in value.  As
hitherto they had been worth only about fifteen
cents on the dollar; as upon the publication of the
secretary's report they had risen to fifty cents on
the dollar; and as, if the secretary's advice should
be taken, they would rise to a hundred cents on the
dollar, — it would be securing what in the slang
of the modern stock exchange is called "a good
thing" to send agents into the rural districts in
advance of the news to buy up government paper.
"My soul rises indignant," exclaimed a member,
"at the avaricious and moral turpitude which so
vile a conduct displays."  Nor on that point did
anybody venture then to disagree with him openly.

But, besides the question as to who were in
reality the public creditors, a doubt was also raised
whether the debt ought to be paid in full to anybody.  Every dollar of the foreign debt was for
an actual dollar borrowed.  But the domestic debt

was not incurred to any large amount for money
borrowed, but in payment for services, or for provisions and goods purchased, for which double,
or more than double, prices had been exacted by
those who exchanged them for government paper.
If the exigencies of war had compelled the government to promise to pay for fifty bushels of wheat
the price of a hundred bushels, the creditor, now
that the government was in a condition to redeem
its promise, was not entitled in equity to receive
more than the actual value of the fifty bushels at
the time of the purchase. Moreover, it was contended, there was no injustice in such a settlement
of the debt, for the war had been carried on and
brought to a successful end, for the benefit of the
creditor as well as of everybody else. The argument was analogous in a measure to that used by
a certain class of politicians in our time, who maintained that the bonds of the United States, bought
at a discount for " greenbacks " during the late
rebellion, should not be redeemed in gold when
the war was over.

The answer to all this was obvious. The nation
must first be just by paying its debts to those
who could present the evidence that they were its
creditors. If, when that was done, it could afford
to be generous, it might, if so disposed, reimburse
those who had lost by parting with the certificates
of debt at a discount. The government could not
in honor go behind its own contracts. The Constitution provided that " all debts and engagements,

entered into before the adoption of this Constitution, shall be as valid against the United States under this Constitution as under the Confederation." Here was a debt which the Confederation had contracted, and the federal government had no more right "to impair the obligation of contracts" for its own benefit than the separate States had; and that they were expressly forbidden by the Constitution to do.

Madison listened quietly day after day to the long and earnest debates upon the subject, and then advanced an entirely new proposition. He agreed with one party in maintaining the inviolability of contracts. The Confederacy had incurred a debt to its own citizens which the new government had agreed to assume. But he also agreed with the other party that there was a question as to whom that debt was due. Were those who now held the certificates entitled to the payment of their face value, dollar for dollar, although the cost to them was only somewhere from fifteen to fifty cents on the dollar? It was true that the original contract was transferable, and these present creditors held the evidence of the transfer. But did that transfer entitle the holder to the full value without regard to the price paid for it? Was there not in equity a reserved right in the original holder, who, having given a full equivalent for the debt, had only parted with the evidence of it, under the compulsion of his own poverty, and the inability of the government at that time to meet

its obligations? Was not this specially true in
the case of the soldiers of the late war, to whose
devotion and sacrifices the nation owed its existence?

Mr. Madison thought that an affirmative reply
to the last two queries would present the true view
of the case, and he proposed, therefore, to pay both
classes of creditors, — those who now held the evidence of indebtedness, acquired by purchase at no
matter what price; and those who had parted with
that evidence without receiving the amount which
the government had promised to pay for services
rendered. It was not, however, to be expected
that the entire debt should be paid in full to both
classes. That was beyond the ability of the government. But it would be an equitable settlement,
he contended, to pay the present holders the highest price the certificates had ever reached, and to
award the remainder to those who were the original
creditors.

This proposition received only thirteen votes out
of forty-nine. Many of those opposed to it were
quite ready to grant that it was hard upon the vet-
erans of the war that they, who had received so
little and who had borne so much, should not now
be recognized as creditors when at last the government was able to pay its debts. But the House
could not indulge in sentimental legislation. That
would be to launch the ship of state upon another
sea of bankruptcy. There were in the hands of
the people tens of millions of paper money not

worth at the current rate a cent on the dollar. If everybody who had lost was to be paid, the point would soon be reached where nobody would be paid at all. A limit must be fixed somewhere; let it be at these certificates of debt which were the evidence of a contract made between the government and its creditors. These could be paid, and they should be paid, to those who were in lawful possession of them. The law, if not the equity, of the case was clearly against Madison. That the government should be absolutely just to everybody who had ever trusted to it, and lost by it, was impossible. It was a bankrupt compelled to name its preferred creditors, and it named those whom it was in honor and law bound to take care of, and over whose claims there was, on the whole, the least shadow of doubt. That the loss should remain chiefly with the soldiers of the Revolution, and the gain fall chiefly to those who were shrewd enough, or had the means to speculate in the public funds, was a lamentable fact; but to discriminate between them was not within the right of the government. That he would have had it discriminate was creditable to Madison's heart; it was rather less creditable to his head.

Of course, underneath all this debate there lay other considerations than those merely of debtor and creditor, of moral and legal obligation, of pity for the soldiers, and of strict regard for the letter of a contract. Mr. Hamilton and his friends, it was said, were anxious to establish the public

credit, not so much because they wished to keep
faith with creditors as because they wished to
strengthen the government and build up their own
party. The reply to these accusations was, that
the other side, under pretense of consideration for
the soldiers and others on whom the burden of the
war had borne most heavily, concealed hostility to
the Constitution and a consolidated government.
These were not reflections to be spoken of in
debate, but they were not the less cherished, and
gave to it piquancy and spirit. There was truth
on both sides without doubt.

Though defeated in this measure, Madison was
not less determined in his opposition to the assumption of the debts of the States. Of these
debts some States had discharged more than
others; and he complained, not without reason, of
the injustice of compelling those which had borne
their own burdens unaided to share in the obligations which others had neglected. He was unfortunate, however, in assuming a superiority for
Virginia over some of the Eastern States, and
especially over Massachusetts, in services rendered
in the struggle for independence. The comparison provoked a call for official inquiry; and that
proved that Massachusetts alone had sent more
men into the field during the war than all the
Southern States together. It was not much to
be wondered at, when this fact was considered,
that the debt of Massachusetts should be larger
than that of Virginia by $800,000. The difference

between Virginia and South Carolina was the same, the truth being that the war had cost Massachusetts more money to pay her soldiers for the general service, and South Carolina more to repel the enemy upon her own soil, than it had cost Virginia for either purpose. Massachusetts and South Carolina were again found acting together, simply because each of them had a debt — $4,000,000 — larger than that of any other State. The total debt of all the States was about $21,000,000; and as that of North Carolina, Pennsylvania, or Connecticut, when added to the $8,000,000 of Massachusetts and South Carolina, amounted to half, or more, of the whole sum, there was no difficulty in forming a strong combination in favor of assumption. No combination, however, was strong enough to carry the measure on its own merits, notwithstanding its advocates attempted to defeat the funding of the domestic debt of the Federal Union unless the debts of the several States were assumed at the same time.

The domestic debt, however, was at length provided for, and the assumption of the debts of the States was rejected till that bargain, referred to in the preceding chapter, which gave to the Southern States the permanent seat of government, was concluded. It would not have been difficult, probably, to defeat that piece of political jobbery by a public exposure of its terms. Why Madison did not resort to it, if, as seems certain, he knew that such a bargain had been privately made, can only be conjectured.  Perhaps he saw that Hamilton, who was applauded by his friends and denounced by his enemies for his clever management, had, after all, only made a temporary gain ; and that Jefferson, whose defense was that Hamilton had taken advantage of his ignorance and innocence, would not, had he not been short-sighted, have made any defense at all.  For the assumption of the state debts by the general government was only a distribution of a single local burden ; and this was a small price for Virginia and the other Southern States to pay for the permanent possession of the federal capital.

While these questions were pending, another was thrown into the House which was not disposed of for nearly two months.  The debates upon it, Madison said in one of his letters, " were shamefully indecent," though he thought the introduction of the subject into Congress injudicious.  The Yearly Meeting of Friends in New York and in Pennsylvania sent a memorial against the continued toleration of the slave trade ; and this was followed the next day by a petition from the Pennsylvania Society for the Promotion of the Abolition of Slavery, signed by Benjamin Franklin as president, asking for a more radical measure.

" They earnestly entreat," they said, " your serious attention to the subject of slavery ; that you will be pleased to countenance the restoration of liberty to these unhappy men, who alone in this land of freedom are degraded into perpetual bondage, and who, amidst the general joy of surrounding freemen, are groaning in servile subjection; that you will devise means for removing this inconsistency from the character of the American people; that you will promote mercy and justice towards this distressed race; and that you will step to the very verge of the power vested in you for discouraging every species of traffic in the persons of our fellow-men."

The words were probably Franklin's own, and, as he died a few weeks after they were written, they may be considered as his dying words to his countrymen, — counsel wise and merciful as his always was.

A memorable debate followed the presentation of these memorials. Even in the imperfect report of it that has come down to us, the " shameful indecency " of which Madison speaks is visible enough. Franklin, venerable in years, exalted in character, and eminent above almost all the men of the time for services to his country, was sneered at for senility and denounced as disregarding the obligations of the Constitution. But the wrath of the pro-slavery extremists was specially aroused against the Society of Friends, and was unrestrained by any considerations of either decency or truth. In this respect the debate was the precursor of every contest in Congress upon the subject that was to follow for the coming seventy years. The Quakers were the representative abolitionists of that day, and the measure of bitter and angry denunciation that was meted out to them was the same measure which, heaped up and overflowing, was poured out upon those who, in later times, took upon themselves the burden of the cause of the slave. The line of argument, the appeals to prejudice, the disregard of facts and the false conclusions, the misrepresentation of past history and the misapprehension of the future, the contempt of reason, of common sense, and common humanity, then laboriously and unscrupulously arrayed in defense of slavery, left nothing for the exercise of the ingenuity of modern orators. A single difference only between the earlier and the later time is conspicuous; the "plantation manners," as they were called five and twenty years ago, which the Wises, the Brookses, the Barksdales, and the Priors of the modern South relied upon as potent weapons of defense and assault, were unknown in the earlier Congresses.

Mr. Madison and some other members from the South, particularly those from Virginia, opposed the majority of their colleagues, who were unwilling that these memorials should be referred to a committee. "The true policy of the Southern members," Madison wrote to a friend, "was to have let the affair proceed with as little noise as possible, and to have made use of the occasion to obtain, along with an assertion of the powers of Congress, a recognition of the restraints imposed by the Constitution." This in effect was done in the end, but not till near two months had passed, within which time the more violent of the Southern members had ample opportunity to free their minds and exhaust the subject. The more these people talked the worse it was, of course, for their cause. Had Madison's moderate advice been accepted then, and had that example been followed for the next sixty or seventy years, it is quite likely that the colored race would still be in bondage in at least one half of the States. But there was never a more notable example of manifest destiny than the gradual but certain progress of the opposition to slavery; for there never was a system, any attempt to defend which showed how utterly indefensible such a system must needs be. Every argument advanced in its favor was so manifestly absurd, or so shocking to the ordinary sense of mankind, that the more it was discussed the more widespread and earnest became the opposition. Had the slaveholders been wise, they would never have opened their mouths upon the subject. But, like the man possessed of the devil, they never ceased to cry, " Let me alone ! " And the more they cried, the more there were who understood where that cry came from.

In one respect Mr. Madison declared that the memorial of the Friends demanded attention. If the American flag was used to protect foreigners in carrying on the slave trade in other countries, that was a proper subject for the consideration of Congress. " If this is the case," he said, " is there any person of humanity that would not wish to prevent them?"[1] But he recognized the limitations of the Constitution in relation to the importation of slaves into the United States, and the want of any authority in the letter of the Constitution, or of any wish on the part of Congress, to interfere with slavery in the States. On these points he would have a decisive declaration, without agitation, and with as little discussion as possible, and there would have dropped the subject. It only needed, he evidently thought, that everybody, North and South, should understand the Constitution to be a mutual agreement to let slavery altogether alone, when the bargain would be on both sides faithfully adhered to.

This was all very well with the numerous persons who were quite indifferent to the subject, or who thought it very unreasonable in the blacks not to be quite willing to remain slaves a few hundred years longer. But there were two other classes to reckon with, and Mr. Madison was not much inclined to be patient with either of them. To let the subject alone was precisely what the hot-headed

[1] The most serious difficulty in the way of the final suppression of the African slave trade in the present century was, that it could be carried on without molestation in American bottoms, under the American flag. The ruling power in the United States, from 1787 to 1860, was never willing that their own cruisers should meddle with the slavers, and resented as an insult to the flag the search, by the cruisers of other powers, of any vessel under the American flag, though it might be absolutely certain that she had come straight from the coast of Africa, and that her "between-decks" was crowded full of negroes to be sold as slaves in Cuba.

members from the South were incapable of doing
then, as they proved to be incapable of doing for
the next seventy years. On the other hand, all
the petitioners could really hope for was that there
should be discussion. The galleries were crowded
at those earliest debates, as they continued to be
crowded on all such occasions in subsequent years.
Many went to learn what could be said on behalf
of slavery, who came away convinced that the least
said the better. Agitation might disturb the harmony of the Union, which was Madison's dread ;
it might lead to the death of an abolitionist, as it
sometimes did in later times ; but it was sure in
the end to be the death of slavery, though its short-
sighted defenders could never understand why.
They could never be made to see that its most
dangerous foes were the friends of its own household, who could not hold their tongues ; that for
their case all wisdom was epitomized in the vulgar
caution " to lie low and keep dark ; " that the exposure of the true character of slavery must needs
be its destruction, and that nothing so exposed it
as any attempt to defend it. Slavery was quite
safe under the Constitution, as Mr. Madison intimated, if its friends would only leave it there and
claim no other protection.

Advocates are never wanting in any court who
believe that the most effective line of defense is
to abuse the plaintiff. The Quakers, it was said,
" notwithstanding their outward pretenses," had
no " more virtue or religion than other people,

nor perhaps so much." They had not made the
Constitution, nor risked their lives and fortunes
by fighting for their country. Why should they
"set themselves up in such a particular manner
against slavery"? Did they not know that the
Bible not only allowed but commended it, "from
Genesis to Revelation"? That the Saviour had
permitted it? That the Apostles, in spreading
Christianity, had never preached against it? That
it had been — the illustration was not altogether a
happy one — "no novel doctrine since the days of
Cain"? The condition of these American slaves
was said to be one of great happiness and comfort;
yet almost in the same breath it was asserted that
to excite in their minds any hope of change would
lead to the most disastrous consequences, and possibly to massacre. The memorialists were bidden
to remember that, even if slavery "were an evil,
it was one for which there was no remedy;" for
that reason the North had acquiesced in it; "a
compromise was made on both sides, — we took
each other, with our mutual bad habits and respective evils, for better, for worse; the Northern States
adopted us with our slaves, and we adopted them
with their Quakers." Without such a compromise
there could have been no Union, and any interference now with slavery by the government would
end in a civil war. These people were meddling
with what was none of their business, and exciting
the slaves to insurrection. Yet how forbearing
were the people of the Southern States who, not-

withstanding all this, "had not required the assist-
ance of Congress to exterminate the Quakers!"

This was not conciliatory. Those who had been
disposed at the beginning to meet the petitions with
a quiet reply that the subject was out of the jurisdiction of Congress were now provoked to give
them a much warmer reception. They could not
listen patiently to the abuse of the Quakers, and,
though they might acquiesce in the toleration of
slavery, they were not inclined to have it crammed
down their throats as a wise, beneficent, and consistent condition of society under a republican
government. Even Madison, who at first was
most anxious that nothing should be said or done
to arouse agitation, while acknowledging that all
citizens might rightfully appeal to Congress for a
redress of what they considered grievances, was
moved at last to say that the memorial of the
Friends was "well worthy of consideration."
While admitting that under the Constitution the
slave trade could not be prohibited for twenty
years, "yet," he declared, "there are a variety of
ways by which it [Congress] could countenance
the abolition, and regulations might be made in
relation to the introduction of [slavery] into the
new States to be formed out of the western territory."

Gerry was still more emphatic in the assertion
of the right of interference. He boldly asserted
that "flagrant acts of cruelty" were committed in
carrying on the African slave trade; and, while

nobody proposed to violate the Constitution, " that
we have a right to regulate this business is as
clear as that we have any right whatever; nor
has the contrary been shown by anybody who has
spoken on the occasion." Nor did he stop there.
He told the slaveholders that the value of their
slaves in money was only about ten million dollars,
and that Congress had the right to propose " to
purchase the whole of them; and their resources
in the western territory might furnish them with
the means." The Southern members would, perhaps, have been startled by such a proposition
as this, had he not immediately added that " he
did not intend to suggest a measure of this kind;
he only instanced these particulars to show that
Congress certainly had a right to intermeddle in
the business." It is quite likely, had he pushed
such a measure with his well-known zeal and determination, that it would have been at least received
with a good deal of favor; and, as the admirers of
Jefferson are tenacious of his fame as the author
of the original Northwest Ordinance, so Gerry,
had he seriously and earnestly urged the policy
of using the proceeds of the sales of territorial
lands to remunerate the owners of slaves for their
liberation, would have left behind him a more fra-
grant memory than that which clings to him as a
minister to France, and as the " Gerrymandering "
governor of Massachusetts. The debate, however, came to an end at last with no other result
than that which would have been reached at the

beginning without debate, except, perhaps, that the vote in favor of the reports upon the memorials was smaller than it might have been had there been no discussion.

Within less than two years, however, Warner Mifflin of Delaware, an eminent member of the Society of Friends, who was one of the first, if not the first, of that society to manumit his own slaves, petitioned Congress to take some measure for general emancipation. The petition was entered upon the journal ; but on a subsequent day a North Carolina member, Mr. Steele, said that, " after what had passed at New York on this subject, he had hoped the House would have heard no more of it ; " and he moved that the petition be returned to Mifflin and be expunged from the journal. Fisher Ames explained in a rather apologetic tone that he had presented the petition at Mr. Mifflin's request, because the member from Delaware was absent, and because he believed in the right of petition, though " he considered it as totally inexpedient to interfere with the subject." The House agreed that the petition should be returned, and Steele then withdrew the motion to expunge it from the journal.

In the next Congress, eighteen months afterward, the House took up the subject of the slave trade, apparently of its own motion, and a bill was passed prohibiting the carrying on of that traffic from the ports of the United States in foreign vessels. The question was as inexorable as death, and the difference in regard to it then was precisely what it was in the final discussion of the next century which settled it forever. One set of men was given over to perdition if they dared so much as talk; the other set talked all the more, and went to the very verge of the Constitution in act all the more, because they were bidden neither to speak nor to move. Courage was not one of Madison's marked characteristics, but he never showed more of it than in his hostility to slavery.

At the third session of the First Congress, which had adjourned from New York to Philadelphia, where it met in December, 1790, Madison led his party in opposition to the establishment of a national bank, which Hamilton had recommended; and again, as in the adjustment of the domestic debt, he and his party were defeated. He compared the advantages and the disadvantages of banks, and possibly he did not satisfy himself, as he certainly did not the other side, that the weight of the argument was against their utility. At any rate, he fell back upon the Constitution as his strongest position. To incorporate a bank was not, he maintained, among the powers conferred upon Congress. The Federalists, who were beginning to recognize him as the leader of the opposition, were quite ready to accept that challenge. "Little doubt remains," said Fisher Ames in rising to reply, "with respect to the utility of banks." Assuming that to be settled, — whether he meant, or not, that such was the conclusion to be drawn

*Fisher Ames —*

from Madison's argument on that point, — he addressed himself to the constitutional question. If the incorporation of a bank was forbidden by the Constitution, there was an end of the matter. If it was not forbidden, but if Congress may exercise powers not expressly bestowed upon it, and if by a bank some of the things which the federal government had to do could be best done, it would be not only right but wise to establish such an agency. This was the burden of the argument of the Federalists, and Madison and his friends had no sufficient answer. The bill was at length passed by a vote of thirty-nine to twenty.

But it had still to pass the ordeal of the cabinet. The President was not disposed to rely upon his own judgment either one way or the other. He asked, therefore, for the written opinions of the secretaries of the treasury and of state, Hamilton and Jefferson, and the attorney-general, Randolph. The same request was made to Madison, probably more because Washington held his ability and knowledge of constitutional law in high esteem than because of the prominent part he had taken in the debate. Hamilton's argument in favor of the bill was an answer to the papers of the three other gentlemen, and was accepted as conclusive by the President.

# CHAPTER XII

MADISON was a Federalist until, unfortunately, he drifted into the opposition. He was swept away partly, perhaps, by the influence of personal friends, particularly of Jefferson, and partly by the influence of locality, — that " go-with-the-State " doctrine, which is a harmless kind of patriotism when kept within proper limits, but dangerous in a mixed government like ours when unrestrained. Had he been born in a free State it seems more than probable that he would never have been President; but it is quite possible that his place in the history of his country would have been higher. The better part of his life was before he became a party leader. As his career is followed the presence of the statesman grows gradually dimmer in the shadow of the successful politician.

In the course of the three sessions of the First Congress the line was distinctly drawn between the Federal and Republican (or Democratic) parties. The Federalists, it was evident, had succeeded in firmly uniting thirteen separate States into one great nation, or into what, in due time, was sure to become a great nation. It was no

longer a loose assemblage of thirteen independent
bodies, revolving, indeed, around a central power,
but with a centrifugal motion that might at any
time send them flying off into space, or destroy
them by collisions at various tangents. Those who
opposed the Federalists, however, had no fear of
a tendency to tangents; the danger was, as they
believed, of too much centripetal force, and that
the circling planets might fall into the central sun
and disappear altogether. Even if there were no
flying off into space, and no falling into the sun,
they had no faith in this sort of political astro-
nomy. They were unwilling to float in fixed orbits
obedient to a supreme law other than their own.

There is no need to doubt the honesty of either
party then, whatever came to pass in later years.
Nor, however, is there any more doubt now which
was the wiser. Before the end of the century the
administration of government was wrested from
the hands of those who had created the Union;
and within fifteen years more the Federal party,
under that name, had disappeared. It would not
be quite just to say that they were opposed for no
better reason than because they were in power.
But it is quite true that the principles and the
policy of the Federalists survived the party organization; and they not only survived, but, so far
as the opposite party was ever of service to the
country, it was when that party adopted the federal measures. It was in accordance with the
early principles of Federalism that the republic

was defended and saved in the war of 1860–65;
as it was the principles of the Democratic state-
rights party, administered by a slaveholding oligarchy, that made that war inevitable.

Hamilton said, in the well-known Carrington
letter in the spring of 1792, that he was thoroughly convinced by Madison's course in the late
Congress that he, " coöperating with Mr. Jefferson,
is at the head of a faction decidedly hostile to me
and my administration, and actuated by views, in
my judgment, subversive of the principles of good
government, and dangerous to the union, peace,
and happiness of the country." At first he was
disposed to believe, because of his " previous im-
pressions of the fairness of Mr. Madison's character," that there was nothing personal or factious
in this hostility. But he soon changed his mind.
Up to the time of the meeting of the First Congress there had always been perfect accord between them, and Hamilton accepted his seat in
the cabinet " under the full persuasion," he said,
" that from similarity of thinking, conspiring with
personal good-will, I should have the firm support
of Mr. Madison in the general course of my administration." But when he found in Madison his
most determined opponent, either open or covert,
in the most important measures he urged upon
Congress, — the settlement of the domestic debt,
the assumption of the debts of the States, and the
establishment of a national bank, — he was compelled to seek for other than public motives for

this opposition. "It had been," he declared, "more uniform and persevering than I have been able to resolve into a sincere difference of opinion. I cannot persuade myself that Mr. Madison and I, whose politics had formerly so much the same point of departure, should now diverge so widely in our opinions of the measures which are proper to be pursued."

In the letter from which these extracts are made Jefferson and Madison are painted as almost equally black, though the color was laid the thicker on Jefferson, if there was any difference. Hamilton seemed to think that, if Jefferson was the more malicious, Madison was the more artful. He is accused of an attempt to get the better of the secretary of the treasury by a trick which was dishonorable in itself, and at the same time an abuse of the confidence reposed in him by Washington. Before sending in his message at the opening of the Second Congress the President submitted it to Madison, who, Hamilton declares, so altered it, by transposing a passage and by the addition of a few words, that the President was made to seem, unconsciously to himself, to approve of Jefferson's proposal to establish the same unit for coins as for weights. This would have been to disapprove of the proposal of the secretary of the treasury that the dollar should remain the unit of coinage. The statement rests on Hamilton's assertion; and as he had forgotten the words which made the change he complained of, and as the

message was restored to its original form by the
President when its possible interpretation was
pointed out to him, it is impossible now to judge
whether Madison may not have been quite innocent of the intention imputed to him.  It is plain
enough, however, that Hamilton was sore and disappointed at Madison's conduct, and that he was
quick to seize upon any incident that justified him
in saying, " The opinion I once entertained of the
candor and simplicity and fairness of Mr. Madison's character has, I acknowledge, given way to
a decided opinion that it is one of a peculiarly
artificial and complicated kind." To justify this
opinion, and as an evidence of how bitter Madison's political and personal enmity toward him had
become, he refers in the same letter to Madison's
relation to Freneau and his paper, " The National
Gazette." " As the coadjutor of Jefferson," he
wrote, " in the establishment of this paper, I include Mr. Madison in the consequences imputable
to it."

The story of Freneau need not be repeated here
at length, having been already told in another
volume of this series of biographies.  If there were
anything in that affair, however, for which Jefferson could be fairly called to account, Madison may
be held as not less responsible.  When the charge
was made that he had a sinister motive in procur-
ing for Freneau a clerkship in the State Department, and in aiding him to establish a newspaper,
Madison frankly related the facts in a letter to

Edmund Randolph. He had nothing to deny except to repel with some indignation the charge that he had helped to establish the journal in order that it might " sap the Constitution," or that there was the slightest expectation or intention on his part of any relation between the State Department and the newspaper. Freneau was one of his college friends, a deserving man, to whom he was attached, and whom he was glad to help. There was nothing improper in commending one well qualified to discharge its duties for the post of translator in a government office; and as those duties, for which the yearly salary was only two hundred and fifty dollars, were light, there was no good reason why the clerk should not find other employment for leisure hours.

If Mr. Madison, having said this, had stopped there, his critics would have been silenced. But when he added that he advised his friend with another motive besides that of helping him to start a newspaper, then, as the expressive modern phrase is, he " gave himself away." There is a feeling, common even in those early and innocent days when such things were rare, that the editor, whose daily bread, whether it be cake or crust, comes from the bounty of the man in office or other place of power, — that an editor so fed, and perhaps fattened, is only a servant bought at a price. Madison said that to help a needy man whom he held in high esteem was his "primary and governing motive." But he adds: "That, as a

consequential one, I entertained hopes that a free
paper . . . would be an antidote to the doctrines
and discourses circulated in favor of monarchy
and aristocracy; would be an acceptable vehicle of
public information in many places not sufficiently
supplied with it, — this also is a certain truth."
What was this but an acknowledgment of the
essential truth of the charge brought against Jefferson and himself? Not that he might not devoutly hope for an antidote to the poisonous doctrines of monarchy and aristocracy, though in very
truth the existence of any such poison was only
one of the maggots which, bred in the muck of
party strife, had found a lodgment in his brain;
not that it was not a commendable public spirit
to wish for a good newspaper to circulate where it
was most needed; not that it was not a most excel-
lent thing in him to hold out a helping hand to the
friend who had been less fortunate than himself, —
but that, in helping his friend to a clerkship in a
department of the government, his motive was in
part that the possession of a public office would
enable the man to establish a party organ. That
was precisely the point of the charge which he
seems to have failed to apprehend, — that public
patronage was used at his suggestion to further
party ends.

Freneau had intended to start a newspaper
somewhere in New Jersey. Whether or not that
known intention suggested that the project could
be better carried out in Philadelphia, and a clerk-

ship in the State Department would be an aid to
it, the change of plan was adopted and the clerkship bestowed upon him.  The paper — the first
number of which appeared five days after his appointment — was, as it was known that it would
be, an earnest defender of Jefferson and his friends,
and a formidable opponent of Hamilton and his
party.  The logical conclusion was that the man,
being put in place for a purpose, was diligent in
using the opportunities the place afforded him to
fulfill the hopes of those to whom he was indebted.
Madison and Jefferson both denied, with much
heat and indignation, that they had anything to
do with the editorial conduct of the paper.  No
doubt they spoke the truth.  They had to draw
the line somewhere ; they drew it there ; and an
exceedingly sharp and fine line it was.  For it is
plain that Freneau knew very well what he was
about and what was expected of him, and his
powerful friends knew very well that he knew it.
They could feel in him the most implicit confidence as an untamed and untamable democrat, and
one, perhaps, whose gratitude would be kept alive
by the remembrance of poverty and the hope of
future favors.  There was clearly no need of a
board of directors for the editorial supervision
of " The National Gazette," and it was quite safe
to deny that any existed.  The fact, nevertheless,
remained that a seat had been given the editor at
Mr. Jefferson's elbow.

Three months before Madison heard that his

relation to Freneau was bringing him under public censure, he showed an evident interest in the
" Gazette " hardly consistent with his subsequent
avowal of having nothing to do with its management.   In a letter to Jefferson he refers to the
postage on newspapers established by the bill for
the regulation of post-offices, and fears that it will
prove a grievance in the loss of subscribers.   He
suggests that a notice be given that the papers
" will not be put into the mail, but *sent as heretofore*," meaning by that, probably, that they would
be sent under the franks of members of Congress,
or by any other chance that might offer.   " Will
you," he adds, " hint this to Freneau?   His subscribers in this quarter seem pretty well satisfied
with the degree of regularity and safety with which
they get the papers, and highly pleased with the
paper itself."   This was careful dry-nursing for
the bantling which had been provided with so comfortable a cradle in the State Department.

The political casuist of our time may wonder
at the importance which attached to this Freneau
affair.   We are taught that " there were giants in
those days," but we may also remember that in the
modern science of " practical politics " they were
as babes and sucklings.   Madison was making
good his place as a leader of the opposition hardly
second to Jefferson himself.   As with Hamilton,
so with the Federalists generally, he fell more
even than Jefferson fell in their esteem.   He fell
more, because he had farther to fall.   No man

had been more earnest than he for a consolidated government; no one had shown more activity to bring about a convention to frame a federal Constitution; and when at last that work was done, no one, not even Hamilton himself, was more zealous to convince his countrymen that national salvation depended upon union, and that union was hopeless unless the Constitution should be adopted. The disappointment and the shock were all the greater when he gradually drew off from those who had hitherto counted him as on their side. They could not understand how he could find so much to oppose in the legitimate administration — as they believed it to be — of a Constitution he had done so much to create, and the beneficent results of which he had foreseen and foretold. Or, if they understood him, it was on the supposition that he had thrown his convictions and his principles to the winds, abandoned his old friends and attached himself to new ones, from motives of personal ambition. This, of course, may not have been absolutely just. It is quite possible that he did not deliberately surrender his principles, but persuaded himself that he was as true as ever to the Constitution. It is, nevertheless, certainly true that the men with whom he was now acting were the men who, having failed to prevent the adoption of the Constitution, now aimed, by zealous endeavors for an assumed strict construction, to defeat the purpose for which it was framed.[1]

[1] "I reverence the Constitution," said Fisher Ames in debate,

Naturally his motives were suspected, and his conduct narrowly watched. Jefferson's influence over him was known to be great, and Jefferson had had nothing to do with the framing of the Constitution, had been doubtful at first of its wisdom, and gave his assent to it at last with many doubts. The Anti-Federal party was growing gradually stronger in Virginia as in all the Southern States; most of Madison's warmest personal friends, as well as Jefferson, were of that party. What chance would he have in the public career he had marked out for himself if his path and theirs led in opposite directions? How much he was influenced by these considerations it is impossible to tell; perhaps he himself could not have told. Perhaps they were not even considerations, but only unconscious influences, which he would have thrown behind him had he recognized them as possible motives. To others, however, whether justly or not, they were quite sufficient to explain his course, and, once accepted, no other explanation was sought for. The appointment of Freneau to office at Madison's request, followed by the almost immediate appearance of a violent party organ,

" and I readily admit that the frequent appeal to that as a standard proceeds from a respectful attachment to it. So far it is a source of agreeable reflection. But I feel very different emotions when I find it almost daily resorted to in questions of little importance. When by strained and fanciful constructions it is made an instrument of casuistry, it is to be feared it may lose something in our minds in point of certainty, and more in point of dignity."

edited by this clerk in Mr. Jefferson's department, was quite enough to raise an outcry among the Federalists; and Madison's explanation, when it came to be known, of his share in that business, did not add to his reputation either for frankness or political rectitude. Perhaps it was at first more the seeming want of frankness that disgusted his old friends. They could have more readily forgiven him had he openly declared that he had gone over to the enemy, instead of professing to find in the Constitution sufficient ground for hostility to their measures. These constitutional scruples they sometimes thought so thin a disguise of other motives as to be better deserving of ridicule than of argument.

All he said and did was watched with suspicion. In the interval between the First and Second Congresses, he and Jefferson made a tour through some of the Eastern States, as they said, for relaxation and pleasure. But it was looked upon as a strategic movement. Interviews between them and Livingston and Burr in New York were reported to Hamilton as "a passionate courtship." They visited Albany, it was said, "under the pretext of a botanical excursion," but in reality to meet with Clinton. Botany naturally suggests agriculture, and as they continued on their journey into New England they were accused of " sowing tares " as they traveled. Such treachery would have been considered as aggravated by hypocrisy had it been known then that on his return Mr. Madison wrote to his father

from New York: "The tour I lately made with
Mr. Jefferson, of which I have given the outlines
to my brother, was a very agreeable one, and carried us through interesting country, new to us
both." This was cool, if the journey really was a
political reconnoissance.

Though Mr. Madison may have been for a time
a special target for this kind of partisan rancor, it
was by no means confined to him. Jefferson had
a very pretty talent for exasperating his enemies,
and nobody could long divide with him the distinction of being the best hated man in the country.
A curious instance of it was given when the question was discussed, both in the First and Second
Congresses, as to the successor to the presidency in
case the office should become vacant by the deaths
of both President and Vice-President. A bill was
sent down from the Senate to the House providing,
in case such a thing should ever happen, that the
president *pro tempore* of the Senate, or, should the
Senate have no temporary president, the speaker
of the House of Representatives, should succeed
to the vacant office. The House sent back the bill
with an amendment substituting the secretary of
state for the succession in the possible vacancy
instead of the presiding officers of the two houses
of Congress. Madison was very earnest for this
amendment, but the Senate rejected it, and the
House finally assented to the original bill. It was
shown in the course of the debate that according
to the doctrine of chances the office of president

would not devolve, through the accident of death, upon a third person oftener than once in about eight hundred and forty years. The rejection of the amendment naming the secretary of state as the proper person to succeed to the presidency, in the improbable event supposed, was nevertheless resented by the Republicans as a direct reflection upon Mr. Jefferson. Nor did the Federalists deny it. With grim humor they seized upon the opportunity, apparently, to announce that not with their consent should he ever be president, even by accident, though he should wait literally eight hundred and forty years. It was a long-range shot, but there could not have been one better aimed.

If before there had been some room for hope, Madison's course in the Second Congress left no doubt as to which party he had cast his lot with. His hostility to the establishment of a bank was, he thought, justified by what he saw at the opening of the subscription books in New York. The anxiety to get possession of the stock was not to him an evidence of public confidence, and an argument, therefore, in favor of such an institution, but "a mere scramble for so much public plunder." He could only see that "stock-jobbing drowns every other subject. The coffee-house is in an eternal buzz with the gamblers." "It pretty clearly appears also," he said, "in what proportions the public debt lies in the country, what sort of hands holding it, and by whom the people of the United States are to be governed." Here, perhaps, was one cause of his hostility to Hamilton's financial policy. Its immediate benefit was for that class whose pecuniary stake in the stability of the government was the largest. This class was chiefly in the Northern States, where capital was in money and was always on the lookout for safe and profitable investment. At the South, capital was in slaves and land, and could not be easily changed. If the Bank and the bondholders were to exercise — as he feared they would, and as he believed that the Federalists meant they should — a controlling influence over the government, it was certainly pretty apparent "by whom the people of the United States were to be governed." It would be the North, not the South; and he was a Virginian before he was a Unionist.

Perhaps he was influenced by this consideration when he proposed that the payment of the domestic debt should be divided between those who had originally held, and those who had acquired by purchase, the certificates of indebtedness. The public creditors would in that case have been more widely distributed in different sections of the country and among different classes. The thought, at any rate, does not seem to have been a new one when he saw and reported the eagerness with which the bank stock was sought for, denounced it as stock-jobbing and gambling, and indignantly reflected that in these men he saw the future governors of the country, and particularly of his own people. No doubt there was a good deal of specu-

lation ; and, as at all such times, there were a few
who made fortunes, while many, who had at first
much money and no stock, next much stock and no
money, had at last neither stock nor money.    But
Mr. Madison's indignation was quite wasted, and
his fears quite unfounded.    Neither the stock-job-
bers, the Bank, nor the bondholders ever usurped
the government, whatever may have been Hamilton's hopes or schemes, if he had any other than
to serve his country.    The money-power of the
North built cities and ships, factories and towns,
and stretched out its hands to the great lakes and
over the broad prairies, to add to its dominion,
to extend its civilization, and to give to labor and
industry their due reward.    It was the South that
devoted itself to the business of politics, and, united
by stronger bonds than can ever be forged of gold
alone, soon entered into possession of the government, which it retained and used for its own interests, without regard to the interests or the rights of
the North, for nearly three quarters of a century.
Mr. Madison had no prescience of any such future
in the history of the country, nor, indeed, then
had anybody else.    He may have really believed
that the holders of a large public debt and the
owners of a great national bank, through which
the monetary affairs of the country could be controlled, were aiming to lay hold of the government.
If all this were true, imminent peril was impending
over republican institutions.    The inconsistency of
which Hamilton accused Madison was therefore not

necessarily a crime.  It might even be a virtue, and
Madison be applauded for his courage in avowing a
change of opinion, if he saw in the practical application of Hamilton's principles dangers that had
not occurred to him when looking at them only
as abstract theories.  But the Federalists believed
that Madison, governed by these purely selfish motives, sacrificed his convictions of what was best
for the country that he might secure for himself a
position on what he foresaw was the winning side.
It is quite likely that the more pronounced enmity
he showed towards Hamilton during the second session of Congress was due in some measure to his
knowledge of this feeling towards himself among
Federalists.  He seemed, at any rate, to be ani-
mated by something more than the proverbial zeal
of the new convert.  If it was not always shown
in debate, it lurked in his letters.  Anything that
came from the secretary, or anything that favored
the secretary's measures, was sure to be opposed
by him.  He was not, of course, always in the
wrong, and sometimes he was very right.  There
was a manifest disposition on the part of the Federalists in the House to defer to the secretary in a
way to provoke opposition from those who did not
share in their estimate of his great ability.  There
was some resentment, for example, when it was
proposed that Congress should submit to the secretary the question of ways and means to carry on
the Indian war at the West, after St. Clair's disastrous defeat, and when, a few days later, it was

suggested that he should be called upon to report a plan for the reduction of the public debt. Members, chief among them Madison, thought that they were quite capable of discharging the duties belonging to their branch of the government without instructions from a head of department whom many of them looked upon as only an official subordinate of Congress. For the same reason they refused with prompt decision to permit the secretary to appear upon the floor of the House to explain some proposed measure. In the Carrington letter Hamilton said that he had " openly declared " a " determination to treat him [Madison] as a political enemy." He probably took care that Madison should hear of it, for he was not a man who made idle threats. He was sometimes arrogant and overbearing in manner, was always ready for a fight, which he rather preferred to quietude, and had little disposition to spare an enemy. These were not conciliating qualities likely to temper the asperities of political warfare, and they may have provoked even Madison, mild-mannered and almost timid as he was, to unusual heat.

All this, of course, is aside from the question whether the party, to which Mr. Madison had given his allegiance, was right or wrong. On that point there may be an honest difference of opinion. It is apart also from the question whether a man may not honestly change sides in politics, notwithstanding the suspicion that always follows him who runs from one side to the other, when in neither has

there been any change in principles or measures.
It is quite possible that he may be governed by the
most sincere convictions; and if he obeys them
and abandons old friends for new ones, or con-
sents to be friendless, it is the strongest proof the
statesman or politician can give of a moral courage
which ought to gain for him all the more respect.
But whether that respect must be denied to Mr.
Madison, because he was governed by other and
lower motives, is the question.   There had been no
change of political principles either in the party he
had left or the party he had joined ; but each was
striving with all its might to adapt the old doctrines to the altered condition of affairs under the
new Union.   The change was wholly in Mr. Madison.   That which had been white to him was now
black; that which had been black was now as the
driven snow.   Why was this?   Had he come to
see that in all those years he had been wrong ?   Or
had he suddenly learned, not that he was wrong,
but that he had mistaken a straight and narrow
path for the broad road which would lead to the
goal he was seeking?   These are not pleasant questions.   He had served his country well; one does
not like to doubt whether it was with a selfish
rather than a noble purpose.   But of any public
man who changed front as he changed, the question always will be, What moved him ?   Not to ask
it in regard to Madison is to drop out of sight
the turning-point of his career ; not to consider it

is to leave unheeded essential light upon one side
of his character.   For his own fortunes the choice
he made was judicious, if to " gain the whole
world " is always the wisest and best thing to do.
He gained his world, and was wise and virtuous
in his generation according to the vote of a large
majority.   Whether that decision still holds good
it is not so easy to say ; probably it does, however ;
for the popular estimate of men often remains un-
changed long after the judgment upon the events
which gave them celebrity is completely reversed.
But history, in the long run, weighs with even
scales ; and the verdict on Madison's character
usually comes with that pitiful recommendation to
mercy from a jury loath to condemn.   Admiration
for his great services in the Constitutional Convention and after it, when its work was presented
to the people for their approval, has never been
withheld ; upon his official integrity and his high
sense of honor in all his personal relations, except
when obligation to party may have overshadowed
it, there rests no cloud ; and his intellectual power
is never questioned.   One having these recognized
qualities, and who for five and twenty years was
generally high in office, must needs be held in
high estimation, especially in a new country where
fame, like everything else, is cheap.   Nevertheless,
impartial historians, who venture to believe that
nature admits of imperfections in a native of Virginia, declare their conviction that Mr. Madison

either wanted the strength and courage to resist
the influence of those about him, or that the ambition of the politician was strong enough to overcome any consideration of principles that might
stand in his way.

# CHAPTER XIII

IF any proof were wanting of how completely
Madison had gone over to the opposition, he gave
it in the memorable attack upon the secretary of
the treasury in the spring of 1793, within four
days of the close of the second session of the Second Congress. It was hoped by that proceeding
to overwhelm Hamilton with disgrace, and that
the President would feel himself obliged to expel
him from the cabinet. When the resolutions with
this aim were offered, a member said that delicacy,
decency, and every rule of justice had been violated; "a more unhandsome proceeding he had
never seen in Congress;" he might have remained
a member to this day, and, save for the attempts
in our time to expel John Quincy Adams and
Joshua R. Giddings, not have changed his opinion.

In the course of the preceding year Hamilton,
under various signatures, had met his opponents
in the newspapers. But it was a veil, not a visor,
behind which he fought; for everybody knew
from whom came the vigorous blows that he dealt
about him right and left. It was a boast always
of Jefferson that he never condescended to news-

paper controversy; but it was pretty well understood that he himself did not enter upon that
rather unsatisfactory mode of warfare because he
preferred the safer method of fighting by proxy.
Hamilton never was in doubt as to who was his
real antagonist, and he aimed his blows over the
heads of his petty assailants to where he knew
they would hit home. They left bad bruises upon
his colleague in the cabinet. Among other papers
of the time, though not a newspaper article, was an
official letter to the President, in which Hamilton
defended his principles and his measures. Early
in 1792 the President, longing to escape the toils
of public life and to spend the rest of his days in
tranquillity, had consulted Madison and his two
secretaries, Jefferson and Hamilton, upon the propriety of his declining a reëlection. He soon
changed his mind, influenced, perhaps, as much by
the dissensions, so evident in the expostulations of
his friends, as by the expostulations themselves.
He deprecated this open feud between his secretaries as a public misfortune, and sought, if he
could not reconcile them, to silence it. That the
Federalists were monarchists, as Jefferson and
Madison never ceased asserting, he knew was not
true, without the emphatic and indignant declara-
tions of Hamilton, Adams, and other leading men
of that party, when they condescended to notice a
charge which they deemed so absurd that it was
difficult to believe that anybody could make it in
earnest. But, while he knew there was no real

danger from that quarter, he could not fail to see that the reverence and love in which he was held constituted a bond of unity, so long as he remained chief magistrate; and he may have felt that, should he retire, there was no other common tie strong enough at that moment to hold together a Union, the possible dissolution of which was, both at the North and at the South, considered with calmness, sometimes with complacency, and, when party passion was at a red heat, even as a thing to be prayed for. At any rate, the President consented to take the advice of the counselors whom he had consulted; but in asking that advice he unwittingly aggravated the quarrel among them which caused him so much uneasiness.

Jefferson, in the arguments he set forth both in conversation and by letter to influence Washington's decision, dwelt upon the unhappy condition of public affairs. It was a storm which he himself meant to get out of by retiring to Monticello, though he thought it was Washington's duty to remain at the helm and keep an eye to windward. This unhappy condition of affairs, he said, had all come from the course pursued by the secretary of the treasury, and was the natural consequence of the acts of Congress in relation to the public debt, the Bank, excise, currency, and other important measures passed in accordance with the secretary's policy. Whether this policy was meant to destroy the Union, subvert the republic, and establish a monarchy upon its ruins, at any rate

such must be the inevitable result of those mischievous measures.  He urged this view of the
subject with such pertinacity that Washington,
either because he was impressed by so much earnestness, or because he was curious to know how
the assertions could best be answered, sent them
to Hamilton, with other objections of a similar
character from other persons, and asked for a
reply.  No names were given, but it is not likely
that Hamilton was at any loss in guessing where
such strictures upon his administration of affairs
came from.  " I have not fortitude enough," he
said in his answer, " always to hear with calmness
calumnies which necessarily include me as a principal object in the measures censured, of the falsehood of which I have the most unqualified con-
sciousness. . . . I acknowledge that I cannot be
entirely patient under charges which impeach the
integrity of my public motives or conduct.  I feel
that I merit them in no degree, and expressions of
indignation sometimes escape me in spite of every
effort to suppress them."  There were only two
men in the country whom he could have had in
mind when he wrote such words as these.  In all
Washington's career there is nowhere a stronger
proof of his strong will, self-reliance, and passion-
less impartiality than that he could stand between
two such furnaces as Hamilton on one side and
Jefferson and Madison on the other, both glowing
at the intensest white heat, while he remained
usually as calm and as unmoved as if breathing

the softest, balmiest, and gentlest airs of a day in
June. But all this personal controversy in the
public prints, and in the official intercourse of the
cabinet, left on both sides an intense exasperation,
which could not fail to have a controlling influence
in the conduct of political parties. Whether Jefferson was conscious or not — and whatever his
feeling was, Madison shared it with him — that in
this paper warfare he was signally defeated, the
attempt to ruin Hamilton by an attack upon him
in Congress followed, if it was not the consequence
of, the mortification of defeat.

In February, 1793, Mr. Giles, a representative
from Virginia, offered a series of resolutions calling upon the President for certain information
relating to the finances. They were a bold attack
upon the secretary of the treasury, and, should it
prove that they could not be satisfactorily answered,
would convict him of mismanagement of the financial affairs of the government, of a disregard of
law, of usurpation of power, and even of embezzle-
ment of the public funds. Any reasonable ground
for believing such charges to be well-founded would
be quite sufficient to bring the secretary to trial
by impeachment. There was probably little doubt
at the moment as to whence this blow came; for
though the hand might seem the hand of Esau, the
voice was the voice of Jacob. Behind Giles was
Madison; and behind Madison, of course, was Jefferson. ' Mr. John C. Hamilton, in his " History
of the Republic," asserts that the resolutions were

still — when he wrote, twenty-five years ago — in
the archives of the State Department at Washington, in Madison's handwriting; and he further declares that Giles assured Rufus King that Madison
was their author.

Hamilton's reply, so far as any intentional
wrong-doing was imputed to him, was conclusive.
There had been technical violations of acts of Congress in one instance, but it was only to carry out
the acts themselves. Congress had, three years
before, passed two acts authorizing the negotiation
of two loans, one for twelve million dollars for the
discharge of the foreign debt, and another for two
million dollars to be used at home. It had been
convenient, and had conduced to the success of the
negotiation, to offer in Holland to contract a loan
for fourteen million dollars, without the unnecessary, and to foreigners probably the confusing,
statement that the authority for borrowing that
amount was derived from two separate acts of Congress. It was only in this borrowing of the money
that there was any seeming disregard of the letter
of the law. The loans and their purposes were
kept entirely distinct in the accounts of the department. Other questions touching the management
of these loans were so clearly and frankly explained
that nothing but the captiousness of party could
refuse to be satisfied. On one point — the charge
of an alleged deficit — the opposition was absolutely silenced. The secretary indignantly explained that the sum — as anybody could have

known for the asking from any officer in the
Treasury Department — which was made to appear as missing was in credits for customs bonds
not yet due, and bills of exchange on Europe sold
but not yet paid for.

Though there was enough of decency, or of prudence which took the place of decency, to drop the
insinuation that the secretary had stolen what had
never been in his possession, it was not so with
the rest of the accusations. Only four days before
Congress was to adjourn, Giles offered another set
of resolutions. These assumed that the defiance
of law and unwarranted assumption of power,
which, at first, were only suggested by the inquiries, were now proved to be true by the explanations that had been given. The indictment,
therefore, was made to include the verdict and
the sentence; the criminal was accused, was to
be found guilty, and condemned to capital pun-
ishment in one proceeding, without the privilege
of trial, or a recognition of the right to be heard.
The argument of the resolutions was, that certain
acts were a violation of law; that the secretary
had committed all those acts ; and therefore it
was the will of the House that the facts be reported to the President. The presumption obviously was, that the President would immediately
dismiss from office a disgraced and faithless public
servant. But the prosecution was an utter failure.
The largest vote received for any of the resolutions was only fifteen ; that on the others was

from seven to twelve, in a quorum of from fifty
to sixty members.    In the course of the debate
Mr. Madison had said that "his colleague [Giles]
had rendered a service highly valuable to the legislature, and no less important and acceptable to the
public."   The House showed by its votes how very
far it was from agreeing with him.   But Fisher
Ames wrote about that time: "Madison is become a desperate party leader, and I am not sure
of his stopping at any ordinary point of extrem-
ity."   If it be really true that he instigated this
attack upon Hamilton, and was the author of the
resolutions, using Giles as his tool to get them
before the House, Ames's reflection was not un-
charitable.

It would not be just, however, to leave the impression that the hostility shown in this affair was
purely personal.   Both Jefferson and Madison had
a hearty hatred for Hamilton which would have
been greatly gratified could they have made it
the plain duty of the President to put him out of
the Treasury Department a dishonored and ruined
man.    But this particular outbreak of their enmity was intensified by their sincere and earnest
enthusiasm for France.   They were quite willing
to bring Hamilton to grief at any time because
he was Hamilton; they were more than ordinarily exasperated against him just now because in
recent newspaper and other controversies he had
altogether got the better of them; but in this
particular instance they wanted to punish him

because of delay of payments in discharge of
the indebtedness of the United States to France.
This was the essential delinquency at which the
Giles resolutions were pointed. The difficulty was,
not that the secretary of the treasury was not
careful enough of the public money, but that he
was too careful. He insisted upon being quite
certain, when paying off a public debt, that he
was paying it to the right persons, and that no
risk should be incurred of its being demanded a
second time. He felt there was no such certainty
about payments to France. The king was de-
throned; but it was not wise, the secretary thought,
to be hasty in recognizing revolutionary governments. It was a republic to-day; it might be a
regency to-morrow; a monarchy again the third
day. It was more prudent to await a reasonable
period for the evidence of permanency on one side
or the other. Those old enough to remember the
late war of the rebellion know how important
the maintenance of this doctrine was in regard to
the recognition of the rebel confederacy by England and France.

But to all this Jefferson did not in the least
agree; neither did Madison. They were in full,
even passionate, sympathy with the men who
brought Louis XVI. to the guillotine. Money,
they knew, was needed, and it was a crime against
liberty to delay payment when payment was due
to the French government. With Hamilton the
question was, not whether the revolutionists ought

to be, but whether they were, France.  With Jefferson and Madison they were France, because they ought to be.  Hesitation to acknowledge that the Revolution was the nation, they thought, could only come from an "Anglican party," the "enemies of France and of Liberty," who would lead the American people "into the arms and ultimately into the government of Great Britain," — to use the terms in which Madison spoke, a little later, of the Federalists.  Which of these men, in this regard at least, were the thoughtful and prudent statesmen, and which were *doctrinaires*, nobody now, probably, questions.  The larger proportion of the people, however, were then carried away by the enthusiasm for the French revolutionists.  It was so, no doubt, at first without much distinction of party ; but it was inevitable, when the government should be called upon to take some decisive stand in relation to European politics, that the country should divide into two hostile camps ; or, rather, that the two camps already existing should become more hostile to each other than ever.  It is not necessary to assume that the mass of the people gave themselves up to any very hard thinking about the matter.  For the most part they followed, as the way is with parties, the political leaders to whom they were already accustomed, never doubting that not to do so would be treacherous to the gratitude America owed to France, and to the cause of liberty and democracy, which, in the hands of the Frenchmen,

was hurling monarchs from their thrones — at least
one monarch from his, and more, it was hoped,
would follow. But when the revolution ran into
the terrible excesses of a later stage, if any Federalists had wavered in their allegiance to their
chiefs they soon returned, persuaded that the wild
and bloody anarchy of Paris was not the road that
led to the establishment of a wise and safe popular
government.

There was no need now of pretexts for quarreling; real causes came fast enough. France declared war against England, and the United States
had its part to play in this strife of giants. Its
real interest was to keep out of trouble; and, if all
were agreed on that point, it does not seem that
there should have been much difficulty in saying
so. "It behooves the government of this country," wrote Washington to Hamilton, "to use
every means in its power to prevent the citizens
thereof from embroiling us with either of those
powers, by endeavoring to maintain a strict neutrality." It is difficult to conceive of a man being
sincerely desirous of helping neither one side nor
the other; of injuring neither one side nor the
other; of maintaining, so far as help or harm
could go, an attitude of absolute impartiality
towards both, — it is difficult to conceive of such
a man quarreling with the word "neutrality" as
applied to his position. But Jefferson, nevertheless, quarreled with it; not frankly and directly
as a thing he did not want, but captiously and

hypercritically objecting to the word to cover his
dislike to the thing itself. "A declaration of
neutrality," he said, "was a declaration that there
should be no war, to which the Executive was not
competent."

It was true that the Executive was not competent to declare that there should be no war; it was
not true that the use of the word "neutrality"
could have any such application to the future as to
prevent Congress, when it should assemble, from
declaring war should it see fit to do so. But
meanwhile, Congress not being in session, and no
exigency having arisen that made it desirable in
the President's judgment to call an extra session,
he, with the assent of the cabinet, — for Jefferson
did not venture upon direct opposition, — issued a
proclamation "to exhort and warn the citizens of
the United States carefully to avoid all acts and
proceedings whatsoever" that might interfere with
"the duty and interest of the United States" to
"adopt and pursue a conduct friendly and impartial towards the belligerent powers." The objectionable word was left out in deference to Mr.
Jefferson, who, really preferring that there should
be no proclamation at all, hoped to take the sting
out of it by the omission of a phrase. It was the
thing said, not the way of saying it, that the President insisted upon, as it was his duty to preserve
the peace till the legislature should declare for
war, and his inclination to preserve it altogether.

It can hardly be doubted that Jefferson and his

friends saw as plainly as the other party saw how
perilous to the interests of the United States a
foreign war would probably be. But, while professing a desire to avoid it, they were far more
anxious, apparently, to give aid, moral as well as
material, to France, with whose revolutionary
struggles they sympathized so deeply, than they
were to avoid offense to England, whom they
hated and would gladly see crippled. Not to be an
enemy of England they held was to be an enemy
of France; and not of France merely, but of the
"rights of man." They could not or would not
comprehend any wisdom in moderation, any prudence in delay. It is curious to see how party
animosity blinded even the best of them. The
objection to the word "neutrality" was a mere
quibble; for the proclamation called upon all good
citizens to maintain at their peril that state which,
in all dictionaries, neutrality is defined to be. Mr.
Jefferson, in instructing as secretary of state the
American ministers abroad as to the attitude assumed by the government, could find no better
term than "a fair neutrality." The fact was, the
Republican leaders wished to avoid taking any
positive stand, partly because delay might be a
help to France, and partly in obedience to the law
of party politics, in opposition to the other side.
They were not at first quite sure of their ground,
and wanted to gain time. Mr. Madison seems to
have waited about six weeks before he could venture upon a positive opinion as to the proclamation.

The newspapers helped him to a knowledge of
party opinion, and party opinion helped him to
make up his own.   " Every ' Gazette ' I see," —
he wrote in June, about eight weeks after the
proclamation was published, — " every ' Gazette '
I see (except that of the United States [Federal-
ist]) exhibits a spirit of criticism on the Anglified
complexion charged on the Executive politics.  . . .
The proclamation was, in truth, a most unfortunate
error."   A week before, he had been seemingly
cautious even in writing to Jefferson.   Then he
had observed that newspaper criticisms aroused
attention, and he had heard expressions of surprise " that the President should have declared
the United States to be neutral in the unqualified
terms used, when we were so notoriously and unequivocally under eventual engagements to defend
the American possessions of France.   I have heard
it remarked, also, that the impartiality enjoined
on the people was as little reconcilable with their
moral obligations as the unconditional neutrality
proclaimed by the government is with the express
articles of the treaty."   He adds: " I have been
mortified that on these points I could offer no
*bona fide* explanations that might be satisfactory."
He was not in doubt long, however.   Mr. Jefferson sent him within two or three weeks a series
of papers by Hamilton, under the signature of
" Pacificus," in defense of the proclamation, and
urged him to reply.   This Madison undertook to
do at once, and in five papers, under the signature

of " Helvidius," he took up all the points in dis-
pute.

The question relating to treaty obligations was
the more serious. By the treaty of 1778 the
United States had guaranteed " to his Most Christian Majesty the present possessions of the Crown
of France in America." An attempt on the part
of Great Britain to take any of the French West
India Islands would involve the United States in
the war. How, then, Mr. Madison's friends might
well ask, as in the letter just quoted he said
they did, could " the President declare the United
States to be neutral in the unqualified terms used,
when we were so notoriously and unequivocally
under eventual engagements to defend the American possessions of France " ? Hamilton's ground
was that the treaty, by its terms, was "a defen-
sive alliance," and therefore not binding in this
case, inasmuch as the present war against England
was offensive; and that, besides, the treaty was
in suspension, as France herself was, in a sense, in
suspension, having only a provisional government,
the permanent and legitimate successor to which
was uncertain. But an important point was
gained, it was thought, in the decision to receive
Genet as the French minister. Hamilton, still
acting in accordance with that cautious policy
which he thought to be, in such a crisis, the most
judicious, questioned whether a minister from the
provisional government in Paris should be recognized without reservations. Such an ambassador

might be followed presently by another accredited by a new power in the revolutionary progress. This would, at the least, be an awkward dilemma not to be recovered from without the loss of some dignity by the government of the United States. But this point also was yielded in deference to Jefferson, and much to his mortification the concession turned out to be before he was many weeks older.

"I anxiously wish," Madison wrote to Jefferson, "that the reception of Genet may testify what I believe to be the real affections of the people." He was amply gratified. From Charleston, where he landed, to Philadelphia, Genet was received with the warmest enthusiasm by all who sympathized with France, and by that larger number among Americans who are always ready to hurrah for anything or anybody that has caught the popular fancy. Madison watched his progress with great interest, and apparently with some misgivings. Writing again a few days later to Jefferson, he says that "the fiscal party in Alexandria was an overmatch for those who wished to testify the American sentiment." Indeed, he thinks it certain, he says in the same letter, "that Genet will be misled if he takes either the fashionable cant of the cities or the cold caution of the government for the sense of the public," — falling himself, before he reaches the end of the sentence, into the cant of assuming neutrality in the government to be only a "mask" behind which to hide

its " secret Anglomany." But he was quite mistaken in supposing that Genet was likely to be
misled, or led at all, by anybody. He was almost
capable, as General Knox said, of declaring the
United States a department of France, and of levying troops here to reduce the Americans to obedience. The man's conduct, if it had not been
so outrageous, would have been ludicrous in its
assumption of power, its disregard of the laws of
the country, and its defiance of the government.
Within three months of his arrival Jefferson himself was constrained to acknowledge that he had
developed " a character and conduct so unexpected
and so extraordinary as to place us in the most
distressing dilemma, between our regard for his
nation, which is constant and sincere, and a regard
for our laws, the authority of which must be maintained; for the peace of our country, which the
executive magistrate is charged to preserve; for its
honor, offended in the person of that magistrate;
and for its character, grossly traduced in the con-
versations and letters of this gentleman." Though
this was in an official letter, it gave, no doubt,
Jefferson's real opinion; for no man had more
reason than he for resenting the conduct of the
irrepressible Frenchman. Jefferson has been accused of too much familiarity with the French minister in private, and of tardiness in the discharge
of his own duty as secretary where it was likely
to clash with the other's schemes. Genet himself
complained that he was thrown over by Jefferson

after receiving from him every encouragement.
This is, of course, true, but not in the least dis-
creditable to Jefferson.  When Genet arrived in
Philadelphia, he was, although he had already
committed some illegal acts in Charleston, profuse
in his promises of good behavior.  The secretary
of state had welcomed him as the representative
of France and the Revolution, and naturally he
meant to make the most he could out of him, for
the sake of the Republican party, as well as for the
sake of the sacred cause of " liberty, equality, and
fraternity."  But he soon saw that he was dealing
with one who was a cross between a mountebank
and a madman, as we learn from a letter of Madison to Jefferson, written within two months of
Jefferson's first interview with Genet.  " Your
account of Genet," says the letter, " is dreadful.
He must be brought right if possible.  His folly
will otherwise do mischief which no wisdom can
repair."

The mischief dreaded was that the administration party would take advantage of the insolent
and outrageous conduct of the French minister
to show the folly of precipitancy, and to gain
popularity and strength for itself.  Madison soon
writes to Jefferson to acquaint him with the reac-
tion taking place in Virginia, " in the surprise and
disgust of those who are attached to the French
cause, and who viewed this minister as the instrument for cementing, instead of alienating, the two
republics."  He asserts that " the Anglican party

is busy, as you may suppose, in making the worst of everything, and in turning the public feelings against France and thence in favor of England." In a sense this must have been true. The "fiscals," the "Anglomanys," the "Anglican party," the "monarchists," — which were Mr. Madison's pet names for his old friends, — were good enough politicians to take great satisfaction in keeping well stirred and in lively use the muddy waters into which their opponents had floundered. They were not, probably, careful always to remember that France was neither the better nor worse, neither the wiser nor the less wise, because one of the mad fanatics, bred of the Revolution, had found his way, unfortunately, to the United States as a minister plenipotentiary. But, on the other hand, it was not true that there was any "Anglican party," in the sense in which Madison used the term, — a party led by men who were "the enemies of France and of liberty, at work to lead the well-meaning from their honorable connection with those [the French people] into the arms and ultimately into the government of Great Britain." Washington said that he did not believe there were ten men in the United States, whose opinions deserved any respect, who would change the form of government to a monarchy. But if there were only ten men in the country whose opinions, in the estimate of Jefferson and Madison, were not worth much, Washington was among them. The affection and reverence, with which he was regarded by

the people, they would have been glad to appeal
to on behalf of their own party; but it is easy to
read between the lines in Jefferson's "Ana," and
in his and Madison's correspondence, that they
looked upon the President as the dupe of his secretary of the treasury.   Not that they were ever
wanting in terms of respect and even of veneration for the President, but the tone was often one
of pitiful regret almost akin to contempt.

" I am extremely afraid," Madison wrote to
Jefferson, " that the President may not be sufficiently aware of the snares that may be laid for
his good intentions by men whose politics at bot-
tom are very different from his own."   Again he
says, a few days later: " I regret extremely the
position into which the President has been thrown.
The unpopular cause of Anglomany is openly lay-
ing claim to him.   His enemies, masking themselves under the popular cause of France, are play-
ing off the most tremendous batteries on him. . . .
It is mortifying to the real friends of the President that his fame and his influence should have
anything to apprehend from the success of liberty
in another country, since he owes his preëminence
to the success of it in his own.   If France triumphs, the ill-fated proclamation will be a mill-
stone, which would sink any other character and
will force a struggle even on his."   Yet it is certain that Washington was not in the least doubt as
to his own political principles; that he was never
in danger of being inveigled into the betrayal of

those principles, whatever they might be; and that
he was quite capable of due care for his own reputation.

If Madison did not know that these tears over
Washington, if sincere, were quite uncalled for,
Jefferson was not in the least deceived. He
records in his " Ana " that the President, referring
to certain articles that had recently appeared in
Freneau's " Gazette," said that " he considered
those papers as attacking him [Washington] directly; for he must be a fool indeed to swallow
the little sugar-plums here and there thrown out
to him; that in condemning the administration
of the government they condemned him, for if they
thought there were measures pursued contrary to
his sentiments, they must conceive him too care-
less to attend to them, or too stupid to understand
them." Again, some months later, the President,
alluding to another article in Freneau's paper, —
that " rascal Freneau," as he called him, — said
" that he despised all their attacks on him person-
ally, but there never had been an act of the government — not meaning in the executive line only,
but in any line — which that paper had not abused.
He was evidently sore and warm," continues the
candid secretary, " and I took his intention to be,
that I should interpose in some way with Freneau,
perhaps withdraw his appointment of translating
clerk in my office. But I will not do it."

These frank and indignant avowals of feeling
and opinion were not, if we may believe Jefferson,

unusual with Washington, even in cabinet meetings; and it seems hardly likely that Madison, who was on the most friendly and intimate terms with the President, could have been so ignorant of how he felt and thought as to suppose him the mere dupe of designing men. The truth is, probably, that Madison did not, any more than Jefferson, believe this. It was only a bit of party tactics to assume, lest the President should have too much influence over the minds of the people, that, in the hands of the wicked " Anglicists," he was as clay in the hands of the potter. The two friends, whether in writing or by speech they lamented and excused the unhappy position, as they were pleased to call it, of the President, must have appeared to each other like the Roman augurs in Gérôme's picture.

# CHAPTER XIV

## HIS LATEST YEARS IN CONGRESS

GENET was at last got rid of, but the evil that he did lived after him. His presence had provoked an outbreak, to some degree, of the phenomena of the French Revolution, which, however significant they might be in the upheaval of an old monarchical despotism, were an unwholesome growth among a simple people, where one man was as good as another before the law ; where, from the first settlement of the country, all had largely possessed the advantages of a popular government; and where any other than a republican government for the future was wellnigh impossible. For men to address each other as " citizen," as if the word had the new significance in America that it had just gained in France ; to swear eternal fidelity to liberty, equality, and fraternity, as if these were lately discovered rights which had been denied the common people for centuries by kings and nobles, who had always lived in the next street in inconceivable luxury wrung from the blood and sweat of the poor ; to form Jacobin clubs pledged to the suppression of the tyranny of aristocrats in a country where, as Samuel Dexter said of New England,

there was hardly a man rich enough to own a car-
riage, and few so poor as not to own a horse; for
men thus to ape those revolutionary ways, which
meant so much in Paris, may have seemed at the
moment, to sober-minded people, more fantastic
than harmful.   It was harmful, however, insomuch
as it substituted sentiment for common sense, and
made enthusiasm, not reason, the guide of conduct.
A character was given to political conflict which
obtained for years to come.   There was, it is true,
a certain manliness about it in remarkable contrast
with that maudlin sentimentality of our time which
is rather inclined to ask pardon of the rebels of the
late civil war for having put them to the trouble
of getting up a rebellion.   It was a conflict, nevertheless, more of party passion than of principle,
wherein it is impossible to see that either party
was absolutely right, or either absolutely wrong.
The Francomania phase of it disappeared for a
time in John Adams's administration; but it
revived again, and gave intensity and virulence to
the political struggles, in the first decade of this
century.   Then it was that men went about their
daily affairs with cockades on their hats as dis-
tinctive party badges.   In their social as well as
in their business relations they were governed by
party affinities.   Neighbors differing in politics
would hardly speak to each other, and each was
always ready to accept the other's political crooked-
ness as the measure of his possible depravity in
everything else.   They would hardly walk on the

same side of the street; or sail in the same packet;
or ride in the same stage-coach; or buy their gro-
ceries at the same shop; or listen to the preaching
of the gospel from the same pulpit; indeed, if the
preacher was known to have pronounced political
opinions, he was held, by those who did not agree
with him, as one from whose shoulders the clerical
gown should be torn.

Gratitude to France had not yet even become
traditional, and it was intensified by the deepest
sympathy for a people struggling for what, by their
aid, Americans had so recently gained. Added to
this was the old hatred to England, which England
as carefully nursed as if it were her settled policy,
by exciting Indian hostilities on the borders, by
outrages on the high seas, and by an interference
with American commerce, exercised with as little
consideration of the rights of an independent nation
as if the States were still colonies in revolt. Never
did a party find, ready made and close at hand,
so many elements of popularity; and these being
appealed to as Genet appealed to them, it was easy
to set the country in a blaze. When the administration was determined that he should be recalled,
and the Republican leaders were anxious to get rid
of him, as they could not restrain him, Jefferson
opposed, in a meeting of the cabinet, the proposition
to ask for his recall, lest such popular indignation
should be aroused as would enable the French
minister to defy the government itself. The seed
sowed by such a man, on such a soil, bore fruit a

thousand fold for almost a generation.    It is not to
be wondered at that the Federalists could not long
hold their own against a party that did not ask the
people to think, but bade them only to remember
— much, indeed, that ought to be remembered —
and to feel.    That is always so much easier to do
than the other, and it is always so much easier to
appeal effectually to sentiment than to reflection,
that the wonder rather is that the Federalists could
hold their own so long as they did.    All things
were against them but one.    Washington, though
altogether above any partisan bias, as he believed
to be the imperative duty of the chief magistrate
of the nation, conducted his administration by the
principles which distinguished the Federalists.    He
was neither, as he intimated to Jefferson, so care-
less as not to know what was done, nor such a
fool as not to understand why it was done ; and so
greatly was he revered for his exalted character,
so universal was the confidence in his integrity,
sagacity, and sound judgment, that, so long as he
remained President, the party that surrounded him
was immovable as a mountain.    His policy was to
stave off a rupture with England, and, if possible,
to bring that power into pacific and rational relations with the United States.    The government
aimed to keep itself clear of entanglement with all
foreign politics ; to maintain that perfect neutrality
which should violate no treaties, offend no national
friendships, provoke no jealousies, and leave England and France to fight their own battles, content

that the United States should be an impartial spectator.  Thirty years afterward, when the Federal party had ceased to exist under that title, this was announced as the true American policy, and was thenceforth known as " The Monroe Doctrine," though the merit, even of re-discovery, did not belong to President Monroe.

In nine cases out of ten, perhaps in ninety-nine out of a hundred, the wisest statesmanship is the knowledge when and how to compromise.  Certainly that was all John Jay, whom the President sent to England to make a treaty, could do.  The treaty was a bad one ; that is, it was not such an one as any President and Senate would have dared to consent to for the last sixty years ; it was not so good an one as that which Monroe and Pinkney negotiated ten years later, and which President Jefferson, lest it should help England and hurt France, then quietly locked up in his desk without permitting the Senate even to know of its existence ; nor was it so bad as the treaty of peace made with England in 1814.  But it was undoubtedly the best that could be done at the time.  The question was between it and nothing ; and the best its warmest defenders could say was that it was better than nothing.  No treaty meant war ; and war at that moment with England meant ruin.  At least so the Federalists thought, and, so far as human foresight could go, they were probably right.

But never was a treaty more unpopular than

this, when its provisions came to be understood. The government, in delaying to make it public, seemed to fear for its reception, and by that hesitation helped to raise the very doubts it was afraid of. But when it was published the whole South was aroused as one man on finding that the payment for fugitive slaves, who during the war of the Revolution had sought refuge with the British army, was not provided for. Other concessions made to England were, in other parts of the country, deemed not less humiliating and injurious to the national honor than this refusal to pay for runaway negroes. Also, there was a one-sided stipulation relating to commerce in the West Indies, so injurious to American interests that the President and Senate, rather than ratify it, determined to reject the whole treaty and take the consequences. There was hardly a town of any note that did not hold its indignation meeting. Jay was burned in effigy, or the attempt was made so to express the public disapprobation, in more than one of the larger towns. Hamilton, when at a public meeting in New York he tried to explain and defend the treaty, was stoned and compelled to retire. If the more violent opponents of the administration were to be believed, its members, from the President down, and all the leading men of the party supporting it, were bought by "British gold," or were ready without being bought, but from pure original depravity, to betray their own country and help to destroy France. The name of the ingenious inventor of the argument of "British gold," then used for the first time, has unfortunately been lost; but it has stood the test of a hundred years' usage, and is as startling and conclusive to-day as it was a century ago.

There soon came, however, the sober second thought which took into consideration the circumstances under which the treaty was made, the possible and even probable consequences of its rejection, as well as the objections to the treaty itself. After the first excitement had passed away, many thought it worth while to read for themselves what hitherto they had only reviled at the suggestion of others, or from sympathy with the popular clamor. The commercial community, the New York Chamber of Commerce leading the way, came to the conclusion that their rights and interests were reasonably protected ; that to be recognized as a neutral between two such belligerent powers as England and France was a great point gained ; that partial indemnity was better than total loss ; and that the chance of a fairly profitable trade in the future was preferable to the ruin of all foreign commerce. It was universally agreed that peace was better than war ; but there was this difference between the two parties : while one maintained that war was not a necessary consequence of the rejection of the treaty, the other declared it must be inevitable, where there were so many points of collision which could only be escaped by mutual agreement. This was especially true on the frontier, where Indian hostilities were sure to follow, and lead to general war, if the military posts, which should have been given up at the close of the Revolution, should remain longer in the hands of the English.

But, after all, the real question with the Republicans was the influence which a treaty with England might have upon the relations of France and the United States. They detested England for her own sake; they detested her still more for the sake of France. If there had been no question of France in the way they would, perhaps, have been willing, like the Federalists, to consider the relations of England and the United States on their merits, — to remember that the commerce between them was greater than that which the United States had with any other country, the loss of which might be a disastrous check to her prosperity; that the peoples of the two countries were, after all, of one blood, and that theirs was a common heritage in the institutions, laws, language, and character that distinguished the race; that the quarrel between them was — though it might be the more bitter on that account — a family quarrel, and ought for that reason to be the more speedily settled. But, if England would not remember these things, — as she never has to this day, — if, on the contrary, she chose to be overbearing, contemptuous, insolent, quite regardless of American rights, — as she always has been when she could be so safely, — then it behooved the United States,

inasmuch as she was a young and as yet a feeble
nation, to conciliate this powerful enemy whenever
she could do so consistently with her self-respect,
to avoid giving unnecessary offense or provoking
fresh injuries, and, in the mean while, to nurture
and husband her strength, to keep an accurate
account of all the wrongs that in her weakness she
should be compelled to submit to, and to bide her
time.  These were the principles of the Federalists.
Their aim was, not the good of England, but the
good of the United States.   They were an American party; to them foreign relations were of importance mainly for the influence these might have
upon the prosperity, happiness, and power of their
own country.   They did not forget the gratitude
due to France for the aid she had given to the
struggling colonies, though that aid was given not
so much for love of America as for hatred of England.   The pacific and friendly relations already
established with France they held in due estimation; and their sympathies went out to her people
in full measure in their struggle for a popular
government, so long as that struggle was kept
within the bounds of reason and humanity.   But
sympathy with and gratitude to France did not
blind them to the wisdom and expediency of pacific
and friendly relations with England, provided such
could be established without the sacrifice of their
own prosperity, independence, and national pride.
It was only to add to that prosperity, to gain new
security for that independence, and to build up a

nation of which they and their children, to the latest generation, might well be proud, that they ought to be on good terms with that powerful state with whom they were co-heirs in all the ideas and institutions constituting the civilization that made her great.  They hoped to build up, west of the Atlantic Ocean, " an Inglishe Nation" in its broadest sense, of which Walter Raleigh had hoped that he might live to see the beginning, and which the latest historical writers in England are just now recognizing as the most important part of the modern empire of the English race.

The House of Representatives was not in session when the Jay treaty was ratified by the President and Senate, but Mr. Madison's letters show that he could see in it nothing but evil.   In February, 1796, the ratification by both governments was announced to both houses of Congress, and measures were at once taken by the Republicans in the lower house to render the treaty, if possible, null and void.  A resolution, warmly supported by Mr. Madison, was offered, calling upon the President for copies of the instructions under which Mr. Jay acted, with the correspondence and any other papers, proper to be made public, relating to the negotiation.   The resolution was subjected to a debate of three weeks, but was finally passed.  The request was refused by the President, on the ground that the treaty-making power was, by the Constitution, confided to the President and Senate.   It was on this point mainly

that the debate had turned; and the President, in
support of his opinion as well as that of the Federalists generally, referred to his recollection of
the plain intention of the Constitutional Convention, and to the fact that a proposition, "that no
treaty should be binding on the United States
which was not ratified by law," was "explicitly
rejected." Mr. Madison said a day or two after,
that, while he did not doubt "the case to be as
stated, he had no recollection of it." Of the message itself, he said that it was "as unexpected as
its tone and tenor are improper and indelicate."
But Hamilton, he thought, wrote it, and the President was, as usual, lamented over for having
been taken in. A resolution, however, was finally
passed in favor of the treaty, though by a majority
of three only. The debate upon it was earnest
and long, Mr. Madison leading the opposition.
His disappointment was bitter. "The progress
of this business throughout," he wrote to Jefferson,
"has been to me the most worrying and vexatious
that I ever encountered; and the more so, as the
causes lay in the unsteadiness, the follies, the per-
verseness, and the defections among our friends,
more than in the strength, or dexterity, or malice
of our opponents."

Though the Jay treaty was not — as was said
on a previous page — such an one as the United
States would have acceded to in latter times, the
result proved it to be a wise and timely measure.
Notwithstanding the disturbed condition of affairs

in Europe, its influence upon the United States, and the increasing violence of faction here, the increase for the next ten or twelve years of the commerce, and the consequent growth and prosperity, of the country were greater than the most sanguine supporters of the treaty had dared to hope for. Their immediate expectations that it might be possible to establish better relations with England, without disturbing essentially those existing with France, were, however, signally disappointed. Their opponents were wiser; for they not only measured accurately the indignation of the French by their own, but they took good care that it should not languish for want of encouragement. The French Directory might have been reconciled to the situation had it been plain to them that there was neither an "Anglicized" party nor a French party in the United States, but that the people were united in the determination to maintain, for their own protection, whatever their personal sympathies might be, an absolute neutrality between the belligerent powers. But as they were assured that their friends in America meant also to be their effectual allies, so they believed that those who professed neutrality used it only as a mask for friendship to England.

James Monroe had been received in Paris as American minister, literally as well as morally, with open arms, in that memorable scene when, in the presence and amid the cheers of the National Convention, the president, Merlin de Douai, im-

printed upon his cheeks, in the name of France,
the kiss of fraternity.  Till he was recalled in the
latter days of Washington's administration, Monroe was the representative not so much of the government to which he owed allegiance as of the
faction to which he belonged at home.  He was
not, it is true, unmindful of the hundreds of outrages perpetrated by French naval vessels and privateers upon American merchantmen ; that their
crews were thrown into French prisons, and that
the detention of their cargoes had brought ruin
upon many American citizens ; nor did he neglect
to demand redress.  But he seemed absolutely
incapable of understanding that if there were anything to choose between the insults and wrongs
which America was compelled to submit to from
England and France, it was only in the greater
ability of England to inflict them.  English ships
swept the ocean, and pretexts were never wanting
for overhauling American vessels, stripping them
of some of their men, or confiscating both ships and
cargoes.  France had as many pretexts, and quite
as good a will to enforce them ; but she had fewer
ships, and for that reason, and that only, did rather
less damage.

But however earnest Monroe was in insisting
upon the rights of neutrals, in urging upon the
French ministry the strict observance of treaty
obligations, and in complaining of the constant
injuries done in their despite, there was another
thing about which he was far more earnest.  He

was as anxious to aid the French to baffle, if possible, Jay's negotiations in London as if he were
uncovering a plot against his own government.
When the ratification of the treaty was made
known in Paris, the indignation of the Directory
was hardly kept within bounds. The minister of
foreign affairs notified Monroe that the Directory
considered the stipulations of the treaty of 1778
as altered and suspended in their most essential
parts by this treaty with England. Under any
circumstances the French would, no doubt, have
resented the establishment of friendly relations
between the United States and the old enemy of
France, with whom she at that moment was engaged in a war arousing more than the bitter inherited enmity of the two peoples. But the course
Monroe had seen fit to pursue had done much to
assure the French that the strong party in the
United States, which he represented, would never
permit the virgin republic to be delivered, as it
was assumed the treaty did deliver her, bound and
gagged, into the hands of the power which Jefferson loved to call " the harlot England." The first
enthusiasm of the Revolution was fast growing
into cant in both countries, and the language of
devotion to liberty, equality, and fraternity was
beginning to lose all meaning. But it was easy to
be deceived by the assurances, more significant in
actions than in words, of an official representative,
that the American people, save an Anglicized and
decreasing minority, were the friends, and meant

to be the allies, of France. Of course the French
were all the more exasperated because they had
permitted themselves to be deluded. Monroe was
first rebuked by his own government for neglecting
to do all that might have been done to reconcile
the Directory to a treaty between the United States
and Great Britain; and soon after, his conduct
continuing unsatisfactory, he was recalled.

It is, of course, possible that the French Directory were not misled; that nothing would have
reconciled them to the British treaty; and that
their subsequent course would have been the same
had they believed the American people were desirous to be on good terms with England solely for
their own tranquillity and interest, and not at all
because any large portion of them were at enmity
with France. This, however, would not be a valid
excuse for Monroe's course as a representative of
his government. The only defense for him is,
that he was deceived by his friends at home; they
must share, therefore, the responsibility for his
conduct, inasmuch as they encouraged a man not
over strong in mind or character, and more likely
to be governed by impulse than by good judgment, to abuse the confidence placed in him by the
administration.

From any share in this responsibility, however,
Madison must be relieved. He was in very constant correspondence with Monroe, and kept him
carefully advised as to the progress of the treaty.
No man desired its defeat more earnestly than he,

and he believed that a majority of the people
were opposed to it. But he evidently doubted its
rejection from the first, and his discussion of possibilities in his letters to Monroe was always frank
and discriminating. In the end he accounted for
the vote in its favor in the House of Representatives by the activity and influence of its friends,
which its opponents wanted the ability or the time
to overcome. It is probable that his colleagues of
his own party in the House did not agree with him
that public opinion was against the treaty, as it
was by votes from their side that its acceptance
was carried.

With the ensuing session of Congress, at the
close of Washington's administration, Madison's
congressional service ended. The leadership of
the opposition, whatever may be thought of its
influence upon the welfare of the country, or of
the personal motives by which he may have been
governed, had devolved upon him, almost from the
beginning, by natural selection of the fittest for
that position. It was not an easy place to take,
either by one's own choice or by the suffrages of
others; for at the head of the administration to be
opposed stood the man most revered by a grateful
country, surrounded by men among those, at least,
who were best known for their past services and
most esteemed for their ability and character. It
was the more difficult for one whose personal relation to the President was that of the warmest
friendship; to whom the President was accustomed

to turn for counsel and even for guidance; and
who, being among those eminent men to whom the
people owed their new Constitution, was counted
upon to strengthen the union of the States and
build up a strong and stable government. He
played his difficult part, nevertheless, with dignity; if not brilliant, he was always ready with the
best reasons that could be given for the measures
he supported; and his zeal was invariably tempered
with a wise moderation and a courtesy toward opponents which made him always respected, and
sometimes feared for reserved force, in debate.

Somewhat more than a year before his retirement from Congress Mr. Madison had married,
and it is quite possible that this may in part have
moved him to seek rest in the tranquillity of a
country life. Tradition says that Mrs. Madison
was a beautiful woman. She has in our time been
a marked figure in the society of Washington, and
many remember her for her fine presence, her
powers of conversation, and that beauty which
sometimes belongs to the aged, though it may not
have been preceded by youthful comeliness. Her
maiden name was Dolly Payne, and her parents
were members of the Society of Friends. When
Madison married her she was Mrs. Todd, the
widow of John Todd, a lawyer of Philadelphia.
Her age at this time was twenty-six years, Mr.
Madison being forty-three, and she survived him
thirteen years, dying in 1849. On her tombstone
she is called " Dolley ; " but Mr. Rives, in his life

of her husband, ever mindful of the proprieties, calls her " Dorothea," or rather, Mrs. Dorothea Payne Madison ; for, like the Vicar of Wakefield, he loved to give the whole name.

## CHAPTER XV

MR. MADISON, in retiring for a time from public office, did not lose his interest in public affairs. Of few Americans can it be said with more truth that he had a genius for politics, and the subject, wherever he might be, was never out of his mind. There is not much else in the volumes of his published letters, while there is just enough else to show that in these he said all he had to say about anything. His more ambitious writings, the papers in "The Federalist," the essay on The British Doctrine of Neutral Trade, his controversial articles in the newspapers under various pseudonyms, are all political, all able, and all of great value as a part of the history of the times. Those which are controversial, however, must be taken, like his letters, as aids to knowledge rather than as definite conclusions to be accepted without question. It does not detract from the value of these letters, however, that they are written from the point of view of a party leader. Affairs of only temporary importance sometimes loom up before him merely because of their influence upon some immediate party movement; and others, of far-reaching consequences, which have no such bearing, escape his notice altogether; but the reader soon learns that he may, at any rate, confide in the sincerity of the writer, and accept as freely the reasons given for his course as they are frankly stated.

Of the literary value of his writings, aside from their historical interest, there is not much to be said, though Mr. Madison always wrote, even in his letters, as if writing for posterity. He was not felicitous in the use of language; the style is turgid, heavy with resounding words of many syllables, unillumined by any ray of imagination, any flash of wit or of humor; and the sentences are often involved and badly put together. But there is a genuineness, an evident sincerity of purpose, in all he wrote, and occasionally an expression of deep feeling, which are always impressive. We search for glimpses of his private life and character in such letters, for they are not easily apparent. In one sense he had no private life, or, at least, none that was not so subordinate to his public career that there was little in it either significant or attractive. There is, in this respect, a marked contrast between his correspondence and that of Jefferson. There was, possibly, a little affectation in Jefferson's frequent assertions of his intense desire for the quiet of the country and the tranquillity of home, and of his distaste for the turmoils and anxieties of public office. But he was certainly fond of country life, with the leisure to potter about among his sheep and his trees; to watch the growth of his wheat and his clover; to contrive new coulters for his plows; to talk of philosophy, of the Social Contract, of mechanics, and of natural history: if he was averse to public life, it was not because political power and distinction were a burden to him, except as they brought with them strife and unpopularity, which truly his soul loathed for himself, though he rather liked to set other people by the ears. His private life was unquestionably as full of interest to himself as it is entertaining to look upon in the unconscious revelation of his own letters.

But with Madison it was apparently quite otherwise. He unbent with difficulty. Always solemn and dignified, it was rather painful than pleasant to him to stoop to the petty matters of every-day existence. He had no small affectations, and was not forever asserting that he was without ambition; as if that, without which nobody is of much use in the world either to himself or to others, were a weakness akin to depravity. With brief intervals, covering only a few months altogether, he was where he best liked to be, from his entrance upon public life in 1775 till he stepped down in 1817 from that political elevation beyond which there are no ascending steps. During these forty-two years he found a certain enjoyment in a country home for a little while at a time, but it was chiefly the enjoyment of needed rest from official labor. The price of tobacco and the promise of the wheat crop interested him then, but only as they inter-

ested him always as a source of his own income,
and as the index to the general prosperity.  At the
end of a letter upon political matters, he announces
with satisfaction that his merino ewe has dropped
a lamb, and both mother and offspring are as well
as could be expected ; but it was probably Mr.
Jefferson's gratification rather than his own that
he had in mind, for it was Mr. Jefferson who had
imported the sheep.   Again, in a similar letter, he
takes a little remaining space to express a hope
that Mr. Jefferson may permit the use of the rams
of that flock to improve the breed of the native
stock ; not, apparently, that he cared so much
about wool as that he wished to show a courteous
and friendly interest in one of Mr. Jefferson's
many projects for the improvement of things generally.

It was probably during the year of comparative
leisure after he left Congress that Mr. Madison
built his house at Montpellier, though some question has been raised on this point.   He certainly
was building a house at that time, and it is not
likely that he ever employed himself in that way
more than once.   Scattered among discussions of
Alien and Sedition Laws, the war in Europe, free
goods in neutral ships, and other public topics,
are brief allusions to lathing nails which he depended upon Mr. Jefferson to supply ; that gentleman having recently set up a machine for their
manufacture, which, however, like a good many
other of his contrivances, seems to have had a

hitch in it.  So also he asks the Vice-President
to see to it that, when the window-glass and the
pulleys are forwarded, the "chord" for the latter
shall not be forgotten; and orders for other articles, only to be found in Philadelphia, are sent
to his obliging friend.  Mr. Jefferson, it is easy
to believe, found them rather the most interesting
part of the political letters to which they were
appended; and he was quite willing, no doubt,
to relieve the tedium of presiding over the Senate
by searching through the Market Street shops for
the latest improvements in builders' hardware.  To
Mr. Monroe, Madison wrote that, as he is sending
off a wagon to fetch nails for his carpenters, "it
will receive the few articles which you have been
so good as to offer from the superfluities of your
stock, and which circumstances will permit me now
to lay in."  Evidently he was getting ready to go
to housekeeping with his young wife.  Monroe's
stock of household goods had been replenished,
perhaps by importations from France on his recent return, and he was disposing of his old supplies, by gift or sale, among his neighbors.  Madison, at any rate, sends this modest list of what
he would like to have: " To wit, two table-cloths
for a dining-room of about eighteen feet; two,
three, or four, as may be convenient, for a more
limited scale; four dozen napkins, which will not
in the least be objectionable for having been used;
and two mattresses."  It was not an extravagant
outfit, even though it had not been meant for

one of those lordly Virginia homes of which some modern historians give us such charming pictures. "We are so little acquainted," — Mr. Madison continues in that stately way which nothing ever surprised him into forgetting, — "we are so little acquainted with the culinary utensils in detail that it is difficult to refer to such by name or description as would be within our wants."

But pots and kettles, — though that may not be the name they were known by in Virginia, — table-cloths and mattresses, however moderate in number, are sure indications that the house, which was to be his residence when he should be content to retire from public service, was finished early in 1798. He had rested long enough, and was busy that year in attendance upon the state Assembly at Richmond, to which he consented the next year to be returned as a member. Perhaps it was because he could not keep longer out of the fray. Perhaps he felt called to a special duty. Affairs, foreign and domestic, were in a critical condition. France, in her resentment at the Jay treaty, had committed so many fresh outrages upon American commerce; had so exasperated the American people by these outrages; and, by refusing to receive the ministers from the United States, had so insulted them and the government they represented in the proposed arrangements, — disclosed in the X. Y. Z. correspondence, — that all friendly relations between the two countries had ceased, and it had seemed impossible that war could be avoided.

For a while the popular sympathy was entirely with Mr. Adams's administration, and the promise could hardly be fairer that the Federalists, if they managed wisely, might remain in power and be sustained by the whole country. But in some respects they were as unwise as in others they were unfortunate. President Adams, though possessing many great qualities, was of too irascible and jealous a temper to be a successful leader or a good ruler. But there were other men of distinction among the Federalists who were hardly less fond of having their own way than the President was of having his. The incompatibility of temper was not altogether on one side in that family quarrel. But all were equally responsible for such a blunder as the enactment of the Alien and Sedition Laws. The provocation, it is true, was unquestionably great. Refugees from abroad had crowded to the United States, many of whom were professional agitators, and some were very sorry vagabonds. Whatever reason they might have had for fomenting discontent with government in England or in France, there was nothing to justify any such violent measures in this country. But from their conduct as political partisans, particularly as newspaper editors, they soon came to be looked upon by the Federalists — for they all joined the other party — as a dangerous class. There grew up a feeling that it would be wiser for civil affairs to remain, in city, state, and nation, in the hands of those who were born and

educated under republican institutions, and not
to fall altogether under control of those who were
alien in blood and religion, and who were inclined to look upon politics, not in the light of
the citizen's duty to the common weal, but as an
easy and profitable calling where the least scrupu-
lous scoundrel could gather the largest share of
spoils.   It may be that the authors of those laws
were so determined to forestall the apprehended
evils of such a dispensation because use had not
accustomed them, as it has later generations of
American citizens, to live under it in humility if
not content.   Or, perhaps, they wanted that pro-
found faith of our time that the longer this sub-
version of government is submitted to, the easier
it will be to get back to the rule of the honest and
wise.

But, at any rate, whatever their reasons, they
meant by these laws relating to aliens to put the
acquirement of citizenship under more stringent
regulations, and to check the growth and promulgation of seditious doctrines.   If it be true, as is
sometimes maintained with some plausibility, that
citizens, to be intrusted with self - government,
should be endowed with a certain degree of intelligence and virtue, then the aim of the framers of
the laws, in the first case, was a good one ; and, in
the second case, the country has had some experience in later times which tends to show that they
were not altogether wrong in believing that doctrines and practices which may lead to insurrection

and civil war might best be met, so far as is possible, at the outset. Nevertheless, the laws, under the circumstances of the time, were ill-considered and injudicious. For one reason, they put an efficient weapon into the hands of the opposition at a moment when it was at a loss where to turn for one. "Anglicism" and "British gold" were blunderbusses which, in the present popular irritation against France, had for a time lost their usefulness, and were apt to miss fire. But an appeal to a generous and impulsive people on behalf of the unfortunate refugees, who had fled from the tyranny of the Old World to find liberty and a home in the New, was sure to be listened to. A good many, besides those who assumed that republicanism and the rights of man were in their special keeping, believed that an unfortunate class had been dealt with hastily, and even cruelly. The clamor, once begun, told heavily against the Federalists. They could be denounced now, not only as the enemies of liberty in France, but as refusing it to men of any nation or any race who should seek it in the United States, — it being, of course, understood that races of black or yellow complexion need not apply. It was, indeed, advanced as an argument against one of the acts, — which gave the President power to order out of the country all aliens whose presence he thought dangerous, — that it might be used to prevent the importation of persons from Africa. On this point Mr. Gallatin, a native of Switzerland, was exceedingly anxious

lest there be a violation of the Constitution. But
the outrage upon the rights of man here apprehended was the right of white men to make black
men slaves.

Against the enactment of these laws Mr. Jefferson did nothing as Vice-President. But whatever
was his motive for official inaction, it was not because he approved them. He wrote the Kentucky
" resolutions of '98," — the strongest protest that
could be made against them, and to be thenceforth
held by nullifiers and secessionists as their cove-
nant of faith. But he acted secretly, taking counsel only with George Nicholas of Kentucky and
William C. Nicholas of Virginia (brothers), and,
Hildreth says, " probably with Madison." The
resolutions were to be offered in the Kentucky
legislature by George Nicholas, and, with some
modifications, were passed by that body in November. A year afterward other resolutions were
passed to reassert the opinions of the previous session, and to record against the laws the " solemn
protest " of the legislature ; and further declaring
" that a nullification by those sovereignties [the
States] of all unauthorized acts done under color
of that instrument [the Constitution] is the rightful remedy." In the resolutions which Mr. Jefferson had prepared for Nicholas the year before, this
essential doctrine is found in that portion which
Nicholas had omitted, in these words, — " where
powers are assumed which have not been delegated,
a nullification of the act is the rightful remedy."

As originally prepared, the resolutions were found
in Jefferson's handwriting after his death.  Hildreth's conjecture that Madison, as well as the
brothers Nicholas, was consulted in the preparation of these resolutions, rests only on circumstan-
tial evidence.  The Kentucky resolutions were
passed in November; those of Virginia in December; the former were written by Jefferson, the
latter by Madison; and the doctrines in each are
essentially the same.  It would have been a perfectly natural thing for the two friends to consult
together upon a measure of so much importance;
there is no reason why they should not have done
so; and these coincidences suggest that they probably did.  Jefferson clearly shirked the responsibility of an act which he knew would endanger the
Union; but Madison made no secret, so far as can
be seen now, of his going to Richmond, though
not a member of the Assembly, apparently for
the express purpose of writing these resolutions
and urging their adoption.  But Jefferson was not
a man of courage even in doing that which he
believed to be wise.  In Madison it was only the
conscience that was timid; and having once convinced himself that the thing he proposed to do
was right, he was always ready to face the consequences.  It may be that neither of them foresaw
that the real importance of this particular act
was rather prospective than immediate; and if
so, their conduct is to be measured by its instant
purpose.  If Jefferson meant then and there to

dissolve the Union, or even to weaken the constitutional bond that held it together, he was not over-cautious in keeping out of sight. But if Madison's intention was to strengthen the Union by withstanding what he believed to be a perilous violation of the Constitution, then his courage, though it is to be commended, is not to be wondered at. That, he said, was his motive, and to defend the resolutions and his own part in regard to them was the chief interest and serious labor of the latter years of his life. He was elected a member of the Assembly for the session of 1799–1800, probably because he and his friends thought his official presence desirable when the subject should again come up for consideration at the reading of the replies from other States, to all which the resolutions had been sent. The report on those replies was also written by him, and the position taken the year before was therein reaffirmed, explained, and elaborated at length.

In 1827–28 the doctrines of nullification and of secession were assumed to be the legitimate corollary of the Kentucky and Virginia resolutions of 1798 and 1799. Jefferson was dead ; but Madison felt called upon to deny, in his own defense and the defense of the memory of his friend, that there was any similarity between them. From 1830 to 1836 his mind seems to have been chiefly occupied with this subject, upon which he wrote many letters, and a paper of thirty pages, entitled " On Nullification," which bears the date of 1835–36, the latter year being the last of his life. He resents the charge of any political inconsistency in the course of his long career, and most of all such an inconsistency as would impugn his attachment to the Constitution and the Union. The resolutions of 1798, he maintains, do not and were not meant to assert a right in any one State to arrest or annul an act of the general government, as that is a right that can only belong to them collectively. Nullification and Secession he denounces as "twin heresies," that "ought to be buried in the same grave." "A political system," he declares, "which does not contain an effective provision for a peaceable decision of all controversies arising within itself would be a government in name only." He asserts that "the essential difference between a free government and governments not free is that the former is founded in compact, the parties to which are mutually and equally bound by it. Neither of them, therefore, can have a greater right to break off from the bargain than the other or others have to hold them to it. . . . It is high time that the claim to secede at will should be put down by the public opinion." What, — he writes to another friend, — "what can be more preposterous than to say that the States, as united, are in no respect or degree a nation, which implies sovereignty, . . . and on the other hand, and at the same time, to say that the States separately are completely nations and sovereigns? . . . The words of the Constitution are explicit, that the Constitution and

laws of the United States shall be supreme over
the Constitution and laws of the several States;
supreme in their exposition and execution, as well
as in their authority.  Without a supremacy in
these respects, it would be like a scabbard, in the
hand of a soldier, without a sword in it." Abra-
ham Lincoln might have said this twenty-eight
years later when he determined that his first duty
as President was to suppress insurrection.

Such is the drift of the many pages Mr. Madison wrote upon the subject during the last five or
six years of his life.  He looked then, whatever
he may have thought in the closing years of the
preceding century, upon the United States as a
nation, and not as a confederacy having its parts
held together only by " a treaty or league " called
a constitution.  But his object is to show that
there is nothing inconsistent in the resolutions of
1798 with these opinions upon the sovereignty
of the United States; that he held them just as
strongly then as he held them now; and that they,
and he as their author, looked to the States as
a whole, not to a single State, to find and apply
a remedy, in a constitutional way, for an unconsti-
tutional measure of which an administration of the
government might be guilty.  His position is maintained with all the acuteness, ingenuity, and logical skill which mark his earlier writings.  There is
no sign of failure of mental power, of which those
accused him who could not answer him.  Such an
imputation he resented with as much indignation

as he did a charge of inconsistency, which here could only mean falsehood. There is no possibility, then, of misunderstanding his opinions during the last six years of his life ; and the world has no right to doubt his repeated and earnest assurances that these were his opinions when he wrote the resolutions of 1798. It can only be said that the construction he gave them thirty years afterward is opposed to the universal understanding of them at the time they were written.

But if his defense of himself be considered complete, it is not even specious when presented on behalf of Jefferson. Mr. Madison wrote in 1830 : "That the term ' nullification' in the Kentucky resolutions belongs to those of 1799, with which Mr. Jefferson had nothing to do. . . . The resolutions of 1798, drawn by him, contain neither that nor any equivalent term." It was not then generally known, whether Mr. Madison knew it or not, that one of the resolutions and part of another which Jefferson wrote to be offered in the Kentucky legislature in 1798 were omitted by Mr. Nicholas, and that therein was the assertion already quoted, — "where powers are assumed which have not been delegated, a nullification of the act is the rightful remedy." The next year, when additional resolutions were offered by Mr. Breckenridge, this idea, in similar though not in precisely the same language, was presented in the words, "that a nullification by those sovereignties [the States] of all unauthorized acts, done under color of that instrument, is the rightful remedy." In 1832, this fact, on the authority of Jefferson's grandson and executor, was made public ; and, further, that another declaration of Mr. Jefferson's in the resolution not used was an exhortation to the co-States " that each will take measures of its own for providing that neither these acts nor any others of the general government, not plainly and intentionally authorized by the Constitution, shall be exercised within their respective territories." All this must have been known to Mr. Madison then, if not before. Yet, three years later, in that paper " On Nullification " which has been mentioned, he wrote : " The amount of this modified right of nullification is, that a single State may arrest the operation of a law of the United States. . . . And this newfangled theory is attempted to be fathered on Mr. Jefferson, the apostle of republicanism." It would be charitable here to believe that there was some lapse of memory in these latter days, and that he had forgotten that Jefferson was, above all things, his own words being witness, the apostle of nullification.

The Alien and Sedition Laws — of which the more obnoxious of the former was never enforced, and the latter expired by limitation in two years — had their influence in the presidential election of 1800. But it was due more to differences between the President and some of the leaders of the Federal party that that party lost its hold upon power, never to be regained. With the election of

Jefferson, Madison entered upon another sphere of
duty, which was politically a promotion, but where
his influence, if it was so large, was not so evident
as when an active leader of his party. It was at
Mr. Jefferson's "pressing desire," Mr. Madison
himself says, in a letter written many years afterward, that he took the office of secretary of state.
In the same letter he explains that he had declined
an executive appointment under Washington, because, in taking a seat in the House of Representatives, he would be less exposed to the imputation
of selfish views in the part he had taken in "the
origin and adoption of the Constitution;" because
there, if anywhere, he could be of service in sus-
taining it against its adversaries, especially as it
was, "in its progress, encountering trials of a new
sort in the formation of new parties attaching
adverse constructions to it." The latter reason
seems to be one of those happy after-thoughts
which public men not unfrequently flatter themselves will anticipate a question they would prefer
should not be asked. Mr. Madison was a member
of the First Congress from the first day it met,
before the new Constitution had encountered new
trials from new parties by any constructions either
one way or the other.

# CHAPTER XVI

## SECRETARY OF STATE

On the morning of March 4, 1801, Mr. Jefferson tied his horse to the fence and walked alone into the Capitol to take the oath of office as President. Mr. Madison was not present at that perfunctory ceremony, the death of his aged father detaining him at home. He soon after, however, assumed the duties of the station to which Mr. Jefferson had called him, and there he remained till he took the presidential office, in his turn, eight years afterward.

The new dynasty entered upon its course under happy circumstances. There was, of course, much to fear from the condition of affairs in Europe; for the United States must needs be in a perilous position so long as the struggle for supremacy continued between France and England, and that would be while Napoleon could command an army. But the danger of war with France was no longer imminent, since Mr. Adams had wisely reëstablished friendly relations, though many of the leading Federalists believed it was at the cost of ruin to his own party. English aggressions upon American commerce had for the moment ceased, as fourteen years afterward they ceased altogether, when the provocation disappeared with the permanent establishment of peace in Europe. In the temporary lull of the tempest the sun shone out of a serene sky, and the land was blessed with quiet and prosperity. "Peace, commerce, and honest friendship with all nations, entangling alliances with none," the President said in his inaugural address, were among "the essential principles of our government, and consequently those which ought to shape its administration." The condition of the country was in accord with the thought and may even have suggested it. "We are all Republicans; we are all Federalists," said Jefferson in his inaugural: it was meant, however, as an avowal of a tolerant belief in the patriotism of both parties, rather than, as has sometimes been supposed, an assertion that party lines, so clearly drawn in the election, were at length obliterated. But hardly a year had passed before this seemed to be almost literally true. One after another, States hitherto Federal, both at the North and at the South, went over in their state elections to the Republican or Democratic party; till, with the exception of Delaware, there was not a single Federal State outside of New England; and even in that stronghold one State, Rhode Island, had marched off with the majority. "Everywhere," wrote Madison in October, "the progress of the public sentiment mocks the cavils and clamors of the malignant adversaries of the administration."

If it may not be asserted that this overthrow of the Federal rule was fortunate at that juncture, — as nothing is more idle in history than speculation upon what might have been, — it may at least be said that Jefferson's administration for his first four years was a happy one for his country and acceptable to his countrymen. None since Washington's has ever been so popular; and no other, except Lincoln's, has ever been so successful. Nor can it be said of it that it was a happy period because it is without a history; for it included acts of moment, accepted then with an approbation and enthusiasm which time has justified. Not less shallow is that view of his character and of those years of his administration, taken by many of his contemporaries, who neither loved nor respected him, and who attributed his success and his popularity to his good fortune. This was a favorite and easy way, among his political opponents, of explaining a disagreeable fact. Parton notes in his Life that C. C. Pinckney could only understand Jefferson's hold upon public confidence as "the infatuation of the people." John Quincy Adams said: "Fortune has taken a pleasure in making Jefferson's greatest weaknesses and follies issue more successfully than if he had been inspired with the profoundest wisdom." "When the people," said Gouverneur Morris, "have been long enough drunk, they will get sober; but while the frolic lasts, to reason with them is useless." There has been more than one occasion of late years, and

in more than one place, where this may be truly
said of popular political enthusiasm; but it was
not true of that which prevailed for the first four
years of this century; and Mr. Adams's sarcasm
can hardly fail to recall the fact that when Mr.
Jefferson, in his second term, was really guilty of
a great folly in adhering to a prolonged embargo,
it was Mr. Adams who committed one of the few
follies of his own life in abandoning his party to
give his support to the President's blunder.

Though there were many changes in Mr. Jefferson's cabinet in the course of eight years, they
were not the result of dissensions. Yet he was,
perhaps, more an absolute President than any
other man who has ever held that position. He
sought and listened to counsel, no doubt; but
taking it was another matter. He certainly did
not take it if it did not suit him; and if it was not
likely to suit him, he was in no hurry to ask for it.
It was in his own fertile brain, not in the sugges-
tions of others, that important measures had their
birth. That trait in his character which phre-
nologists have named secretiveness largely governed his actions. It was natural for him to
bring things about quietly and skillfully by setting others to do what he wanted done, without
himself being seen, though sometimes there was no
other motive than the mere gratification of secretiveness. He preferred often to suggest measures
quietly to congressmen rather than to Congress,
though the result in either case might be the same.

At other times, where the end to be attained was of great importance and he was absolutely sure only of himself, he boldly took the responsibility, as he did in the purchase of Louisiana, and in the suppression of the Monroe-Pinckney treaty with England in his second term. It is not surprising, therefore, that Madison's part, during the eight years of Jefferson's presidency, is found to be more a secondary one than is usual with a secretary of state, or than was usual with him. He was in perfect accord with his chief, who held always in the highest esteem his knowledge and judgment, and sought, no doubt, his sound and moderate advice when he thought he needed advice from anybody. But Madison's influence is less visible in Jefferson's administration than in Washington's, when he was in the opposition. Washington, where he doubted his own ability to decide a question and felt the need of enlightenment, was accustomed to call in Madison, though he did not always accept his friend's conclusions. It was rarely that Jefferson was troubled with any doubt of his own judgment in the discussion or decision of any question that might come before him.

The most important measure of his administration was peculiarly his own, and when once determined upon it was pushed to a conclusion with vigor and courage. Nobody doubts now, or has doubted since the abolition of slavery, that the purchase of Louisiana was an act of sound statesmanship. Jefferson did not foresee that the acqui-

sition of that fertile territory would stimulate a
domestic trade in slaves, as profitable to the slave-
breeding as to the slave-consuming States; or
that, as slavery increased and brought prosperity
and power to a class, there would grow up an
oligarchy, resting on ownership in negroes, which,
within sixty years, would have to be uprooted at
an enormous cost. But his aim was to secure the
peaceful possession of the Mississippi territory on
both its banks, as a permanent settlement of a
question which, so long as it remained open, was a
perpetual menace of war with one or another European power. That danger would always involve
the possibility of the Appalachian range becoming
the western boundary of the United States; in
which case the valley of the Mississippi, and the
vast region west of it, would fall into the power
of an alien people. So far was plain to Mr. Jefferson; but the result of the rebellion of 1861
proves that he was wiser than he knew when he
acquired the territory stretching to the Sabine and
the foot of the Rocky Mountains for the occupation
of a free people.

It is not necessary to repeat here the story of
the purchase. The news of it reached Washington
in July and was received with enthusiasm. That
there was no warrant in the Constitution for an
acquisition of territory by purchase was manifest;
and Mr. Jefferson's opponents were not in the least
backward in heaping reproaches and ridicule upon
the great champion of strict construction, who had

no hesitation in violating the Constitution when it seemed to him wise to do so. Both the President and his secretary frankly met the accusation by acknowledging its entire justice; but at the same time they put in, as a sufficient defense, the plea of the general welfare. This did not abate the ridicule, though the argument was a hard one for the Federalists to withstand; for it could not be forgotten that it was on this ground that Hamilton, as secretary of the treasury, had justified the imposition of certain taxes, and the Republicans had maintained that the plain limitations of the Constitution could not be overstepped on such a plea, even for the general good. Jefferson was so sensitive to this constitutional objection that he proposed to meet it by an amendment to the Constitution; but it was soon evident that the unwritten law of manifest destiny did not need the appeal to the ballot-box. "The grumblers," Jefferson wrote to a friend soon after the news of the treaty was received, "gave all the credit of the acquisition to the accident of war." "They would see," he added, in records on file, "that though we could not say when war would arise, yet we said with energy what would take place when it should arise." He only meant by this, probably, that from the beginning of his administration he had been prepared to take advantage of circumstances when war should break out again between England and France, as it was evident enough to the whole world that it must break out sooner or later. That the particular conjunction of circumstances, however, would occur that did occur, could not have been foreseen. Jefferson could have had no prescience that Spain would reconvey Louisiana to France ; that Napoleon would enter at once upon extensive preparations for colonization on the banks of the Mississippi ; and that he would be willing to relinquish this important step in his great scheme of a universal Latin Empire, that he might devote himself to the necessary preliminary work of subduing his most formidable enemy of the rival race. But it is Jefferson's best title to fame that he was ready to take advantage of this conjunction of incidents at exactly the right moment. Doubtless the progress of civilization would have been essentially the same had he never been born. But having been born it fell to him to contribute largely to the events that have distributed the race speaking the English tongue the most widely over the globe, and to exercise a powerful influence upon the age. It does not detract from the merit of his act, however, that he by no means saw all its importance, nor even dreamed of its consequences. The region beyond the Mississippi, he thought, might be made useful as a refuge for Indian tribes of the East ; but he neither saw nor could see then that the purchase of Louisiana was the essential though only the preliminary step toward the occupation of the continent to the Pacific by the English race. The expedition of Lewis and Clarke, which he sent out the next year, was in the interest of science, and especially of geography, rather than of any possible settlement of that distant region. Indeed, he said that if the new acquisition of territory were wisely managed, so as to induce the eastern Indians to cross the great river, the result would be the " condensing, instead of scattering, our population." But " man proposes and God disposes."

The immediate consequences, however, of the acquisition of Louisiana were enough to bring almost universal popularity to the President, especially at the South and West, without any revelation of the future. Nor was the act the less popular because it was an immediate stimulus to the foreign slave trade, partly because at the North that excited but little interest, and partly because at the South it excited a great deal. The abolition societies, it is true, asked that the importation of slaves from Africa into the annexed territory should be forbidden ; and an act was passed prohibiting their introduction, except by those persons from other parts of the United States who intended to be actual settlers, and were, therefore, permitted to bring slaves imported previous to 1798. But the law might properly have been entitled An Act for the Encouragement of the Trade in Negroes; and so it seems to have been regarded by the older slave States. South Carolina reopened the trade to Africa, and, as Congress failed to levy the constitutional tax of ten dollars a head, the raw material, so to speak, came in free. The rest could be safely left to the law of supply and demand. Neither South Carolina nor any other State had imported slaves since 1798. The whole slave population, therefore, could be legally taken into Louisiana by actual settlers, and its place supplied in the old States by new importations. The demand regulated the supply, and the supply came from Africa as truly as if the importation had been direct to New Orleans. This was the legal course of trade till 1808; thenceforward it flourished, without the protection of law but in spite of it, so long as it was profitable, — so long, that is, as the natural increase of the eastern negro was insufficient to answer the demand of the southwestern market.

But, besides the peaceful extension of the national domain, there was much else in the first four or five years of Jefferson's administration to commend it to his countrymen. His party had nothing to complain of, despite that genial and generous assurance of the inaugural which could not be forgotten, — " we are all Republicans; we are all Federalists;" and the other party had reason to be thankful that, considering, as he said, "a Federalist seldom died, and never resigned," the number was not large who were reminded, by their removal from office, of their unreasonable delay in doing either the one thing or the other. It was only the politicians, however, a class much smaller then than it is now, who were concerned in such matters; the people at large were influenced by other considerations. Credit was given

to the President for things that he did not do, as
well as for things that he did. It was due to him
that the administration was an economical one,
but it was through Mr. Gallatin's skillful management of the finances that the old public debt was
in process of speedy extinction. Occasional im-
peachments enlivened the proceedings of Congress,
which otherwise were as harmless as they were
dull. Jefferson was never so much out of his
proper element as in war, yet a successful one was
carried on, during his first term, with the Barbary
States which put an end for many years to the
exactions and outrages which had long been need-
lessly submitted to. It was a war, however, of
only a few naval vessels in the hands of such ener-
getic and brave men, destined to become famous
in later years, as Bainbridge, Decatur, Preble, and
Barron; and to send off the expedition was about
all the government had to do with it. It was easy
to keep clear of " entangling alliances," or entan-
glements of any sort with European powers, so long
as they left the commerce of the United States to
pursue its peaceful and profitable course without
molestation. This both England and France did
for several years, and there fell, in consequence,
an immense carrying trade into the hands of
American merchants, which brought prosperity to
the whole country such as was never known before,
and was not known again, after it was lost, for
near a quarter of a century. All these things
made Mr. Jefferson acceptable to the people as

almost a heaven-appointed President. If, as John Quincy Adams thought, Fortune delighted to beam upon him with her sunniest smiles, he knew, at least, how best to take advantage of them. While they lasted, his secretary of state sat in their light and warmth, quietly and contentedly busy and in the diligent and faithful discharge of official duty, which could not in those years of prosperous tranquillity be over-burdensome.

# CHAPTER XVII

## THE EMBARGO

ALMOST at the beginning of his second term,
Jefferson found himself in troubled waters, as the
United States was drawn slowly but surely into
the vortex of European war. The carrying trade
at home and abroad had fallen very much into the
hands of Americans, and this became the root of
bitterness. The tonnage of their vessels employed
in foreign trade and entered at the custom-houses of
the United States was equal to nearly four fifths
of the tonnage of British vessels engaged in the
same traffic and entered at home. But there was
this difference: the foreign commerce of Great
Britain was almost all carried on from her own
ports, and the returns, therefore, showed its full
volume. On the other hand, the American ships
were largely the carriers between the ports of the
belligerents and of other powers in Europe, and
there were no entries at the American custom-
houses of their employment, or that they were employed at all. As early as 1804–5, the aggregate
value of this foreign trade in the hands of Americans was probably much larger than that controlled
by English merchants; and the former increased

to the time of the promulgation of the Berlin
decree of 1806, and the British orders in council
of the next year. Nor was it only that wealth
flowed into the country as the immediate return
from this trade abroad. It stimulated enterprise
and industry at home by the increase of capital;
and there was not only more money to work with,
but more to spend. Consequently the increase in
exports and in imports grew steadily. In 1805,
1806, and 1807, about one half the average total
exports, something over the value of twenty million dollars, went to Great Britain alone ; and
the value of the imports from that country for the
same period was about sixty million dollars a year.
Nor did this disproportion, though increasing with
the growing prosperity, represent a general balance of trade against the United States, as one
school of political economists would insist it must
have done. For the imports were small from other
European countries in exchange for American
products ; and the difference, together with the
profits of the carrying trade abroad, was remitted
in English manufactures. In other words, the imports from England represented the returns for all
exports to Europe, and the returns also — available
in the first instance through bills of exchange —
of the trade which had been gained by Americans,
and lost by those nations whose ships the war had
driven from the ocean.

The British manufacturer had no reason for discontent with this state of things. The best market

for his goods was constantly improving, and he did not much care who took them to America. But the English government, and the English merchants who owned ships, looked on with neither pleasure nor patience. It was impossible not to see that the United States was fast becoming a great commercial rival. This in itself was bad enough ; but it was the harder to bear when it was remembered — and it could not be forgotten — that the rivalry came from States so lately in revolt against England, and that their President at that moment was one of the most obnoxious of the rebels. Then what did it avail that England was mistress of the seas, if her formidable enemy could laugh at any effort of hers to destroy the commerce of France, so long as that commerce could be carried on in safety under a neutral flag ? If that flag must be respected, English naval vessels and privateers would cruise in vain for prizes, for the merchant ships of any belligerent, not strong enough to protect them, stayed in port. It had not yet come to be the acknowledged law of nations that free ships make free goods. But nearly the same purpose was answered if the property of belligerents could be safely carried in neutral ships under the pretense of being owned by neutrals. The products of the French colonies, for example, could be loaded on board of American vessels, taken to the United States and reshipped there for France as American property. England looked upon this as an evasion of the recognized public law that property of belligerents was good prize. Accordingly, when she saw that French commerce was thus put out of her reach, and that the rival she most dreaded was growing rich and powerful in the possession of it, she sought a remedy and was not long in finding one.

It was denied that neutrals could take advantage of a state of war to enter upon a trade which had not existed in time of peace; and American ships were seized on the high seas, taken into port, and condemned in the admiralty courts for carrying enemy's goods in such a trade. The exercise of that right, if it were one by the recognized law of nations, would be of great injury to American commerce, unless it could be successfully resisted. To show that it was not good law, Mr. Madison wrote his "Examination of the British Doctrine which Subjects to Capture a Neutral Trade not Open in the Time of Peace." The essay was a careful and thorough discussion of the whole question, and showed by citations from the most eminent writers on international law, by the terms of treaties, and by the conduct of nations in the past, that the British doctrine was erroneous and would lead to other infringements of the rights of neutrals. But argument, however unanswerable, has never yet brought the British government to reason, unless there was something behind it not so easy to disregard. The appropriation for Mr. Jefferson's gunboats could not get that naval arm ready for effective service much before the year 1815, even

if it could then be of use ; and there was, moreover, this further difficulty in the way of its effi-
ciency at the time, — that, as it could not go to the
enemy, it must wait for the enemy to come to it ;
the conflagration would have to be brought to the
fire-engines.   A war with England must be a naval
war; and the United States not only had no navy
of any consequence, but it was a part of Mr. Jefferson's policy, in contrast with the policy of the
preceding administrations, that there should be
none, except these gunboats kept on wheels and
under cover in readiness to repel an invasion.   But
there was no fear of invasion, for by that England
could gain nothing.   " She is renewing," Madison
wrote in the autumn of 1805, " her depredations
on our commerce in the most ruinous shapes, and
has kindled a more general indignation among our
merchants than was ever before expressed."

These depredations were not confined to the
seizing and confiscating American ships under
the pretense that their cargoes were contraband.
Seamen were taken out of them on the charge of
being British subjects and deserters, not only on
the high seas in larger numbers than ever before,
but within the waters of the United States.   No
doubt these seamen were often British subjects
and their seizure was justifiable, provided England
could rightfully extend to all parts of the globe
and to the ships of all nations the merciless system of impressment to which her own people were
compelled to submit at home.   Monroe, in a note

to Madison, said that the British minister had informed him that "great abuses were committed in granting protections" in America, and acknowledged that "he gave me some examples which were most shameful." But even if it could be granted that English naval officers might seize such men without recourse to law, wherever they should be found and without respect for the flag of another nation, it was a national insult and outrage, calling for resentment and resistance, to impress American citizens under the pretense that they were British subjects. But what was the remedy? As a last resort in such cases, nations have but one. Diplomacy and legislation may be first tried, but, if these fail, war must be the final ordeal. For this the administration made no preparation, and the more evident the unreadiness the less was the chance of redress in any other way. Immediate war would, of course, have been unwise; for what could a nation almost without a ship hope from a contest with a power having the largest and most efficient navy in the world? If this, however, was true from 1805 to 1807, it was not less true in 1812. But it need not have been true when war was actually resorted to, had the intervening years been years of preparation. The fact was, however, that the party which supported the administration was no more in favor of war at the earlier period than the administration itself was; and meanwhile, till a war party had come into existence and gained the ascendency, the country had been growing every year less and less in a condition to appeal to war.

The first measure adopted to meet the aggressions of the English was an act prohibiting the importation of certain British products. This had always been a favorite policy with Madison. He had advanced and upheld it in former years, when a member of Congress, and when Great Britain had first violated the rights and dignity of the United States by interference with her foreign trade and by impressing her citizens. Non-intercourse had been an effective measure thirty years before, and had a kind of prestige as an American policy. It was not seen, perhaps could not be seen without experience, that a measure suited to the colonial condition was not sufficient for an independent nation. But the President and secretary were in perfect accord; for Jefferson preferred anything to war, and Madison was persuaded that England would be brought to terms by the loss of the best market for her manufactures. Others, and notably John Randolph, saw in the measure only the first step which, if persisted in, must lead to war; while, in the mean time, to interfere with importations would be quite as great an injury to the United States as to Great Britain. Randolph was apt to blurt out a good deal of truth when it happened to suit him. Impressment, he said, was an old grievance which had been thought a sufficient provocation for war when the nation was not prepared; and it was no more ready to resort to

that desperate remedy now than it had been in the
past. Without a navy it would be impossible to
prevent the blockading of all the principal American ports by English squadrons. The United
States would need an ally, and he was not willing
she should throw herself into the arms of that power
which was seeking universal conquest. France, he
said, would be the tyrant of the ocean if the British navy should be driven from it. The commerce,
moreover, which it was proposed to protect, was
not the " honest trade of America," but " a mush-
room, a fungus of war, — a trade which, so soon as
the nations of Europe are at peace, will no longer
exist." It was only " a carrying trade which cov-
ers enemy's property ; " and he did not believe in
plunging a great agricultural country into war for
the benefit of the shipping merchants of a few
seaports. There were many who agreed with him ;
for it was one of the cardinal principles of the Jeffersonian school of politics that between commerce
and agriculture there was a natural antagonism.

But the administration did not rely upon legislation alone in this emergency. The President
followed up the act prohibiting the introduction
of British goods by sending William Pinkney to
England in the spring of 1806 to join Monroe,
the resident minister, in an attempt at negotiation.
These commissioners soon wrote that there was
good reason for hoping that a treaty would be
concluded, and thereupon the non-importation act
was for a time suspended. In December came the

news that a treaty was agreed upon, and soon after it was received by the President. The most serious difficulty in the way of negotiation had been the question of impressment. The British government claimed the right to arrest deserters from its service anywhere outside the jurisdiction of other nations, and that jurisdiction, it was maintained, could not extend beyond the coast limit over the open sea, the highway of all nations. There was an evident disposition, however, to come to some compromise. The English commissioners proposed that their government should prohibit, under penalty, the seizure of American citizens anywhere, and that the United States should forbid, on her part, the granting of certificates of citizenship to British subjects, of which deserters took advantage. But as this would be an acknowledgment virtually of the right of search on board American ships, and the denial of citizenship in the United States to foreigners, the American commissioners could not entertain that proposition. They were willing, however, if the assumed right to board American ships were given up, to agree, on behalf of their government, to aid in the arrest and return of British deserters when seeking a refuge in the United States. But to this the British commissioners would not accede.

Monroe and Pinkney were enjoined, in the instructions written by the secretary of state, to make the abandonment of impressment the first condition of a treaty. A treaty, nevertheless, was agreed upon, without this provision. But when it was sent to the President, the ministers explained: —

"That, although this government [the British] did not feel at liberty to relinquish, formally, by treaty, its claim to search our merchant vessels for British seamen, its practice would nevertheless be essentially, if not completely, abandoned. That opinion has since been confirmed by frequent conferences on the subject with the British commissioners, who have repeatedly assured us that, in their judgment, we were made as sure against the exercise of their pretension by the policy which their government had adopted in regard to that very delicate and important question, as we could have been made by treaty."

These assurances did not satisfy the President. Without consulting the Senate, though Congress was in session when the treaty was received, and although the Senate had been previously informed that one had been agreed upon, the President rejected it. On several other points it was not acceptable; but, as Mr. Madison wrote to a friend, "the case of impressments particularly having been brought to a formal issue, and having been the primary object of an extraordinary mission, a treaty could not be closed which was silent on that subject." The commissioners, therefore, were ordered to renew negotiations. This they faithfully tried to do for a year, but were finally told by the British minister that a treaty once concluded and signed, but afterward rejected in part by one of the contracting powers, could not again be taken up for consideration. The opponents of the administration made the most of this action of Mr. Jefferson. The country was not permitted to forget, even were forgetfulness possible, that thousands of seamen had been taken from American vessels, and that the larger proportion of these were native-born citizens of the United States. Not that these opponents wanted war; that, they believed, would be ruinous without a navy, and therefore some reasonable compromise was all that could be hoped for. But what was to be thought of an administration that would not go to war because it was not prepared; would not prepare in the hope that some future conjunction of circumstances would stave off that last resort; and, meanwhile, would accept no terms which might at least mitigate the injuries visited upon the sea-faring people of the United States, and possibly relieve the nation from an insolent exercise of power which it was not strong enough to resent?

As England's need of seamen increased, the captains of her cruisers, encouraged by the failure of negotiation, grew bolder in overhauling American ships and taking out as many men as they believed, or pretended to believe, were deserters. In the summer of 1807 an outrage was perpetrated on the frigate Chesapeake, as if to emphasize the contempt with which a nation must be looked upon which only screamed like a woman at wrongs which it wanted the courage and strength to resent, or the wisdom to compound for. The Chesapeake

was followed out of the harbor of Norfolk by the
British man-of-war Leopard, and when a few miles
at sea, the Chesapeake being brought to under the
pretense that the English captain wished to put
some dispatches on board for Europe, a demand
was made for certain deserters supposed to be on
the American frigate. Commodore Barron replied
that he knew of no deserters on his ship, and that
he could permit no search to be made, even if there
were. After some further altercation the Englishman fired a broadside, killing and wounding a
number of the Chesapeake's crew. Commodore
Barron could do nothing else but surrender, for
he had only a single gun in readiness for use, and
that was fired only once and then with a coal from
the cook's galley. The ship was then boarded, the
crew mustered, and four men arrested as deserters.
Three of them were negroes, — two natives of the
United States, the other of South America. The
fourth man, probably, was an Englishman. They
were all deserters from English men-of-war lying
off Norfolk; but the three negroes declared that
they had been kidnaped, and their right to escape
could not be justly questioned ; indeed, the English
afterward took this view of it apparently, for the
men were released on the arrival of the Leopard at
Halifax. But the fourth man was hanged.

For this direct national insult, explanation, apology, and reparation were demanded, and at the
same time the President put forth a proclamation
forbidding all British ships of war to remain in

American waters.　Of how much use the latter was we learn from a letter of Madison to Monroe: "They continue to defy it," he wrote, "not only by remaining within our waters, but by chasing merchant vessels arriving and departing."　Some preparation was made for war, but it was only to call upon the militia to be in readiness, and to order Mr. Jefferson's gunboats to the most exposed ports.　Great Britain was not alarmed.　The captain of the Leopard, indeed, was removed from his command, as having exceeded his duty; but a proclamation on that side was also issued, requiring all ships of war to seize British seamen on board foreign merchantmen, to demand them from foreign ships of war, and if the demand was refused to report the fact to the admiral of the fleet.　It was not till after four years of irritating controversy that any settlement was reached in regard to the affair of the Chesapeake.

New perils all the while were besetting American commerce.　In November, 1806, Napoleon's Berlin decree was promulgated, forbidding the introduction into France of the products of Great Britain and her colonies, whether in her own ships or those of other nations.　This was in violation of the convention between France and the United States, if it was meant that American vessels should come under the prohibition; but for a time there was some hope that they might be excepted. In the course of the year, however, it was officially declared in Paris that the treaty would not be

allowed to weaken the force of a war measure
aimed at Great Britain. Under this decision, cargoes already seized were confiscated and the trade
of the United States faced a new calamity. The
decree, it was declared, was a rightful retaliation
of a British order in council of six months before, which had established a partial blockade of
a portion of the French coast. In the kidnaping
business, France could not, of course, compete
with England; for there were few of her citizens
to be found on board of American vessels, and to
seize a Yankee sailor, under the pretense that he
was a Frenchman, was an absurdity never thought
of. But hundreds of Americans, the crews of ships
seized for violation of the terms of the Berlin decree, were thrown into French prisons. So far,
therefore, as the United States had good ground of
complaint on any score against either power, there
was little to choose between them. Mr. Jefferson's
repugnance to war was sufficient to hold him back
from one with England, though he might have had
France for an ally; still more unwilling was he, by
a war with France, to make a friend of England,
whom he still looked upon as the natural enemy of
the United States; for, notwithstanding all that
had come and gone, he still regarded France with
something of the old affection. In the autumn of
1807 he called a special session of Congress in consideration of the increasing aggressions of Great
Britain, especially in the attack upon the Chesapeake, and the injury done by the interdiction of

neutral trade with any country with which that
power was at war. But he had no recommenda-
tions to offer of resistance nor even of defense,
except that some additions be made to the gunboats, and that sailors on shore be enrolled as a
sort of gunboat militia. The probable real purpose of calling the extra session, however, appeared
in about two weeks, when he sent a special message to the Senate recommending an embargo.

An act was almost immediately passed which,
if anything more was needed to complete the ruin
of American commerce, supplied that deficiency.
A month before this time the English ministry had
issued a new order in council — the news of which
reached Jefferson as he was about to send in his
message — proclaiming a blockade of pretty much
all Europe, and forbidding any trade in neutral
vessels unless they had first gone into some British
port and paid duties on their cargoes ; and within
twenty - four hours of the President's message
recommending the embargo, Napoleon proclaimed
a new decree from Milan, by which it was declared
that any ship was lawful prize that had anything
whatever to do with Great Britain, — that should
pay it tribute, that should carry its merchandise,
that should be bound either to or from any of its
ports. All that these powers could do to shut
every trading vessel out of all European ports was
now done ; and at this opportune moment Mr.
Jefferson came to their aid by compelling all
American vessels to stay at home. It is not easy

in our time to conceive of a President proposing,
or of a party accepting, or of the people submitting to, such a measure as this. But Mr. Jefferson's followers were very obedient, and there was,
undoubtedly, a very general belief that trade with
the United States was so important to the nations
at war that for the sake of its renewal the obnoxious decrees and orders in council would soon be
repealed. But, except upon certain manufacturers
in England, little influence was visible. General
Armstrong, the American minister in France,
wrote: " Here it is not felt; and in England, amid
the more recent and interesting events of the day,
it is forgotten." When, however, the effect was
evident at home of a law forbidding any American
vessels from going to sea, even to catch fish, and
prohibiting the export of any of the products
of the United States, either in their own ships or
those of any other country, then there arose a
popular clamor for the abandonment of a policy
so ruinous. Within four months of its enactment,
Josiah Quincy of Massachusetts declared, in a
debate in Congress, that " an experiment such as
is now making was never before — I will not say
tried — it never before entered into the human
imagination. There is nothing like it in the nar-
rations of history or in the tales of fiction. All
the habits of a mighty nation are at once counter-
acted. All their property depreciated. All their
external connections violated. Five millions of
people are engaged. They cannot go beyond the

limits of that once free country; now they are not even permitted to thrust their own property through the grates." While American ships at home were kept there, those which had remained abroad to escape the embargo were met by a new peril. Some of them were in French ports awaiting a turn in affairs; others ventured to load with English goods in English ports, to be landed in France under the pretense, supported by fraudulent papers, that they were direct from the United States or other neutral country. The fraud was too transparent to escape detection long, and Napoleon thereupon issued, in the spring of 1808, the Bayonne decree authorizing the seizure and confiscation of all American vessels. They were either English or American, he said; if the former, they were enemy's ships and liable to capture; but if the latter, they should be at home, and he was only enforcing the embargo law of the United States, which she ought to thank him for.

The prosperity and tranquillity which marked the earlier years of Jefferson's administration disappeared in its last year. Congress, both in its spring and winter sessions, could talk of little else but the disastrous embargo; proposing, on the one hand, to make it the more stringent by an enforcement act, and, on the other, to substitute for it non-intercourse with England and France, restoring trade with the rest of the world, and leaving the question of decrees and orders in council open for future consideration. The President no longer held his party under perfect control. The mischievous results of the embargo policy were evident enough to a sufficient number of Republicans to secure in February, 1809, the repeal of that measure, to take effect the next month as to all countries except England and France, and, with regard to them, at the adjournment of the next Congress. But the prohibition of importation from both these latter countries was continued till the obnoxious orders in council and the decrees should be repealed.

# CHAPTER XVIII

Mr. Jefferson named his own successor. Of the three Democratic candidates, Madison, Monroe, and George Clinton, he preferred Madison now, and urged Monroe to wait patiently as next in succession. Beyond two lives he did not, perhaps, think proper to dictate; and, besides, Clinton was not a Virginian. What little opposition there was to Madison in his own party came from those who feared that he was too thoroughly identified with Jefferson's policy to untie the knot in which the foreign relations of the country had become entangled. Of the 175 electoral votes, however, he received 122; but that was fewer by 39 than had been cast for Jefferson four years before. Of the New England States, Vermont alone gave him its votes, changing places with Rhode Island, which had wheeled into line again with the Federalists.

During the winter of 1808–9, after Madison's election but before his inauguration, he had quietly conferred with Erskine, the British minister at Washington, upon the condition of affairs. Much was hoped from these conferences; but the

end which they helped to bring about was the
reverse of what was hoped for. Could Madison
have had his way, he would probably have preferred that Congress should have left untouched
at that session the questions of embargo and non-
intercourse; for the tone of the debates and the
tendency of legislation naturally led the English
ministry to doubt the assurances which Erskine
gave that these proceedings did not truly represent
the friendly disposition of the incoming President.
In answer to those representations, however, there
came in April from Canning, the foreign secretary, certain propositions which were so presented
by Erskine, and so received by the administration, as to promise a settlement of all differences
between the two governments. Erskine was a
young man, anxious very likely for distinction;
but a laudable ambition to be of service in a
good cause made him over-zealous. He exceeded
the letter of his instructions, while keeping, as he
thought, to their spirit. Probably he mistook their
spirit in assuming that his government cared more
to secure a settlement of existing difficulties than
for the precise terms and minor details by which
it should be reached. At any rate, he agreed that
Great Britain would withdraw her orders in council provided the United States would maintain the
non-intercourse acts against France so long as the
Berlin and Milan decrees remained in force. This
being secured, he did not insist upon two other
conditions — partly because it was represented to

him that they would need some action by Congress, and partly because he believed that the essential point was gained by an agreement on the part of the United States to enforce non-intercourse against France while her decrees were unrepealed. These other conditions were, first, that the United States should cease to insist upon the right to carry on in time of war the colonial trade of a belligerent which had not been open in time of peace to neutrals; and, second, the acknowledgment that British men-of-war might rightfully seize American merchant vessels when transgressing the non-intercourse laws against France. He also proposed a settlement of the Chesapeake question, but omitted to say, as Canning had instructed him to say, that some provision would be made, as an act of generosity and not of right, for the wives and children of the men who were killed on board that ship. But when that settlement was accepted by the administration, he failed to resent some reflections from Robert Smith, the secretary of state, on the conduct of Great Britain in that affair, which Canning, when he heard of them, thought should have been resented and their recall demanded, or the negotiation stopped.

On the terms, however, as Erskine chose to present them, an agreement was reached, and the President issued a proclamation repealing the acts of embargo and non-intercourse as against Great Britain and her colonies after June 10. On that day more than a thousand ships, loaded and riding at anchor in all the principal ports in anxious readiness for the signal for flight, spread their wings, like a flock of long-imprisoned birds, and flew out to sea. There was an almost universal shout of gratitude to the new President, who, in the first three months of his administration, had banished the fear of war abroad, and at home was sweeping away involuntary idleness, want, and ominous discontent. Madison had known something of popularity during his long career; but never before had he felt the exultation of riding upon the very crest of a mighty wave of popular applause. But it was one of those waves that collapse suddenly into a surprising flatness. Canning repudiated all that Erskine had done and immediately recalled him. The ships that had gone to sea, under the sanction of the President's proclamation, were permitted by an order in council to complete their voyages unmolested; but otherwise all commerce was once more brought to a standstill. It would have been easier to bear some fresh misfortune than to be compelled to struggle again with calamities so well understood and which it was hoped had been left behind forever. Gallatin had been retained in the Treasury Department and was the President's chief adviser, and the two were now accused of having been either imbecile or treacherous. It was openly said that they had led the young minister to agree to an arrangement which they knew his government would not sanction. But they could hardly have been so foolish as to make a bargain with the certainty that it would stand only so long as a ship could go and come across the Atlantic. Nobody understood better than Madison how grateful a reconciliation with England would be to a large proportion of the people, and nobody was more disappointed that the negotiations came to worse than nothing, inasmuch as their failure led to new embarrassments.

He said with some bitterness, in a letter to Jefferson, early in August: "You will see by the instructions to Erskine, as published by Canning, that the latter was as much determined that there should be no adjustment as the former was that there should be one." He was unjust to Canning; the real fault was with Erskine, and with him only because his zeal outran his judgment. In another letter to Jefferson, the President says: "Erskine is in a ticklish situation with his government. I suspect he will not be able to defend himself against the charges of exceeding his instructions, notwithstanding the appeal he makes to sundry others not published. But he will make out a strong case against Canning, and be able to avail himself much of the absurdity and evident inadmissibility of the articles disregarded by him." Possibly Mr. Erskine considered that his government would approve of his not urging these points too earnestly, inasmuch as the other side refrained from insisting upon the abandonment of impressment of seamen on board American ships. But Mr. Madison's

indignation must have covered up a good deal of
mortification. He could hardly have been without
the sensation of one hoisted by his own petard. It
was only two years since Mr. Jefferson, with his
approval, had rejected the Monroe-Pinkney treaty
because instructions had not been literally complied with. Mr. Canning, in following that example, could have pleaded, had he chosen, much the
stronger justification, under the circumstances of
the two cases; and Mr. Madison could not fail to
remember, without being reminded of it, when this
agreement was thrown back in his face, that he
had been willing to accept it without any protection of the rights of American seamen, the want of
which was the ostensible reason for rejecting the
Monroe-Pinkney treaty.

However, the administration was now compelled
to meet anew the old difficulties which the Erskine
agreement had failed to dispose of. The President's first duty was to issue a second proclamation, recalling the previous one which had sent to
sea every American ship in port. They could all
come back, if they would, to be made fast again
at their wharves, till the recurrent tides at last
should ripple in and out of their open seams, and
their yards and masts drop piecemeal upon the
rotting decks. But many never came back, preferring rather the risk of being sunk or burned
at sea, which happened to not a few, or of capture and confiscation by the belligerents whose
laws they defied. Erskine was followed by a new

ambassador from England, Mr. Jackson. His mission, however, had no other result than to widen the breach between the two nations. A controversy almost immediately arose between the minister and Mr. Smith, the secretary of state, — or rather Mr. Madison himself, who, as he complained at a later period, did most of Smith's work as well as his own, — touching the arrangement with Erskine. Jackson intimated, or was understood as intimating, that the administration must have known the precise terms on which Erskine was empowered to treat with the government of the United States; and when a denial was made with a good deal of emphasis on the part of the administration, the insinuation was repeated almost as a direct charge. Of course there could be but one conclusion to correspondence of this sort; further communication with Jackson was declined and his recall asked for.

It was plain enough in the latter months of Jefferson's administration, to himself as well as to everybody else, that the embargo had not only failed to bring the belligerents to terms abroad, but that it had added greatly to the distress at home. That the measure was a failure, Madison himself acknowledged in one of his retrospective letters written in the retirement of Montpellier, sixteen years afterward. It was meant, he said in that letter, as an experimental measure, preferable to naked submission or to war at a time when war was inexpedient. It failed, he added, " because

the government did not sufficiently distrust those
in a certain quarter whose successful violation of
the law led to the general discontent, which called
for its repeal." That is to say, the government
relied too confidently upon the submission of New
England; was too ready to believe that her merchants would not let their ships slip quietly out to
sea whenever they could evade the officers of the
customs, nor slip in to land a cargo at some unfre-
quented place where there was no custom-house.
"The patriotic fishermen of Marblehead," he says,
"at one time offered their services;" and he regrets
they were not sent out as privateers to seize these
contraband ships as prizes, and to "carry them into
ports where the tribunals would enforce the law."
Apparently there was not a reasonable doubt in
his mind whether such tribunals could be found in
any port along the coast of New England. It is
also rather more than doubtful — even assuming
that there was much of the kind of patriotism
which he says existed in Marblehead — how long,
had the government offered commissions to private
citizens to prey upon their neighbors, the embargo
would have been respected at all east of Long
Island Sound. But this was the afterthought of
1826. Madison's policy in 1809–10 was rather to
conciliate than provoke "those in a certain quarter." He could not command entire unanimity
even in his own party. Congress passed the winter
in vain efforts to find some common ground, not
merely for Democrats and Federalists, but for the

Democrats alone. Various measures were proposed to meet the critical condition of the country.
Some were too radical; some not radical enough;
and none were so acceptable that it was not easy
to form combinations for their defeat. All were
agreed that the non-importation act must be got
rid of; but the difficulty was to find a way to be
rid of it so that the nation should at once maintain
its dignity, assert its rights, and escape a war.
The President would have preferred that all British and French ships be excluded from American
ports, and that importations from both countries
should be prohibited except in American vessels;
and a bill to this effect was one of several that was
defeated in the course of the session. But at last,
in May (1810), an act was passed excluding only
the men-of-war of both nations, but suspending the
non-importation act for three months after the adjournment of Congress. The President was then
authorized, when the three months were passed, to
declare the act again in force against either Great
Britain or France, should the commercial orders or
decrees of either nation be continued in force while
those of the other were repealed.

If the aim of the dominant party had been to
devise a scheme sure to lead to fresh complications
more difficult to manage than any that had gone
before, it could not have hit upon a better one
than this. Hitherto, in all the perplexities and
anxieties of the situation, the government had,
at least, kept its relations to other powers in its

own hands, to conduct them, whether wisely or
unwisely, in its own way.   It could resent or submit to encroachments upon the commerce of the
country, as seemed most prudent; it could close
or open the ports, as seemed most judicious; or it
could join forces with that one of its two enemies
whose alliance promised to secure respect on the
one hand, and compel it on the other.   But now
it had tied itself up in a knot of provisos.   It
would do something if England would do something else, or if France would do something else.
If the proposition was accepted by England and
was not accepted by France, then the United
States would remain in friendly relations with
England, and assume by comparison an unfriendly
attitude toward France; and if France accepted
the condition and England declined it, then the
situation would be reversed.   Nothing would be
gained in either case that might not have been
gained by direct negotiation, and, no doubt, on
better terms.   But if the proposition now offered
should be disregarded by both powers, the situation would be worse than before.   This evidently
was Madison's view of the question.   He wrote to
Pinkney, the minister at the Court of St. James,
a month after the act was passed: " At the next
meeting of Congress, it will be found, according
to present appearances, that instead of an adjustment with either of the belligerents, there is an
increasing obstinacy in both; and that the incon-
veniences of embargo and non-intercourse have

been exchanged for the greater sacrifices, as well as disgrace, resulting from a submission to the predatory system in force." Not that he wanted war; his faith in passive resistance was still unshaken; embargo and non-intercourse he was still confident would, if persisted in long enough, surely bring the belligerents to terms. But as to this act, he weighs the chances as in a balance. In England some impression may be made by the prices of cotton and tobacco, — "cotton down at ten or eleven cents in Georgia; and the great mass of tobacco in the same situation." He has, however, no "very favorable expectations." But as to France, he evidently is not without hope that she will be wise enough to see that "she ought at once to embrace the arrangement held out by Congress, the renewal of a non-intercourse with Great Britain being the very species of resistance most analogous to her professed views." But he was clearly not sanguine.

If that was his wish, however, it was gratified. Napoleon did take advantage of the act, but in such a way as to reverse the relative positions of the two nations by seizing for France and taking from the United States the power or the will to dictate terms. The French minister, Champagny, announced in a letter merely, in August, the revocation of the Berlin and Milan decrees from the 1st of the following November; and, a day or two after, such new restrictions were imposed upon American trade, by prohibitory duties and a navigation act, as pretty much to ruin what little there was left of it. The revocation of the edicts, moreover, was coupled with the conditions that Great Britain should not only recall her order in council, but renounce her "new principles of blockade," or that the United States should "cause their rights to be respected by the English." Napoleon had in this three ends to gain, and he gained them all: First, to secure France against a renewal of the non-importation act of the United States, if the President should accept this conditional recall of the decrees as satisfactory; second, to leave those decrees virtually unrepealed, by making their recall depend upon the action of England, who, he well knew, would not listen to the proposed conditions; and, third, to involve the United States and England in new disputes, which might lead to war. Everything turned out as the emperor wished. The President accepted the conditional withdrawal of the French decrees, as in accordance with the act of Congress; England refused to recognize a contingent withdrawal as a withdrawal at all; and the result at length was war between England and the United States.

The acquiescence of the President in the decision of Napoleon was the more significant inasmuch as Mr. Smith, the secretary of state, had assured the French government, when a copy of the act of May was sent to it, that there could be no negotiation under the act until another matter was disposed of. A decree, issued at Rambouillet in

March, 1810, and enforced in May, ordered the confiscation of all American ships then detained in the ports of France, and in Spanish, Dutch, and Neapolitan ports under the control of France. The loss to American merchants, including ships and cargoes, was estimated to be about forty million dollars. This decree was ostensibly in retaliation of that act of non-intercourse passed by Congress more than a year before, and was, therefore, a retrospective law. The non-intercourse act, moreover, had expired by its own limitation months before many of these ships were seized; but all, nevertheless, were confiscated, though some of them had entered the ports merely for shelter. By order of the President, Smith wrote to Armstrong, the American minister at Paris, that "a satisfactory provision for restoring the property lately surprised and seized, by the order or at the instance of the French government, must be combined with a repeal of the French edicts, with a view to a non-intercourse with Great Britain; such a provision being an indispensable evidence of the just purpose of France toward the United States." The injunction was repeated a few weeks later; but when the emperor's decision upon the decrees was announced, in August, the " indispensable " was dispensed with, and a few months later an absolute refusal of any compensation for the spoliation under the Rambouillet decree was quietly submitted to.

But meanwhile the President, in November,

issued a proclamation announcing that France had
complied with the act of the previous May and
revoked the decrees, while the English orders in
council remained unrepealed. But England still
had three months, according to the act, in which to
make her choice between a recall of her orders in
council or the alternative of seeing the American
non-intercourse act revived against her. But, it is
to be observed, the French minister's announce-
ment of the acceptance of the act of May was not
made till August, and then the revocation of the
decrees was not to take effect till November. November came bringing with it the President's proclamation, when it soon appeared that there was
still to be " tarrying in the eating of the cake."
The decrees were to remain in force at least three
months longer, till it should be known whether
Great Britain would comply with those terms which
France — not the United States — made the condition of revoking the orders in council ; and if
Great Britain did not comply, then the French
decrees were not revoked. The legality of the
President's proclamation, of course, was questioned. There was, as Josiah Quincy said in debate in the House, the following February (1811),
" a continued seizure of all the vessels which came
within the grasp of the French custom-house, from
the 1st of November down to the date of our last
accounts." Other members, not more earnest, were
less temperate in the expression of their indignation at what, one of them said, would be called

swindling in the conduct of private affairs; while
another declared that the President was throwing
the people " into the embrace of that monster at
whose perfidy Lucifer blushed and hell stands
astonished." France knew all this while what
England's decision would be. She was ready to
rescind the orders in council when the French
edicts were revoked, but she did not recognize a
mere letter from the French minister, Champagny,
to the American ambassador as such revocation.
The second French condition, that England should
abandon her " new principles of blockade " and
accept in their place a new French principle, was
peremptorily rejected by the English ministry.
That proposition opened a question not properly
belonging to an agreement touching the decrees
and orders, — a question of what was a blockade,
and what could properly be subject to it. Napoleon's doctrine was, not only that a paper blockade
was not permissible by the law of nations, but that
there could be no right of blockade " to ports not
fortified, to harbors and mouths of rivers, which,
according to reason and the usage of civilized
nations, is applicable only to strong or fortified
places." Mr. Emott, a member of the House
from New York, said in debate that the United
States might well be grateful to both England and
France, if they would agree upon this doctrine as
good international law; since in that case, as there
were no fortified places in the United States, she
would never be in peril of a blockade. But it was

precisely what England would not admit nor even discuss as relevant to an agreement to revoke the orders and decrees.

To "this curious gallamatry," as Quincy called it, "of time present and time future, of doing and refraining to do, of declaration and understanding of English duties and American duties," was added another ingredient of Madison's own devising. The American ministers in England and France were instructed that Great Britain would be expected to include in the revocation of her orders in council the blockade of a portion of the coast of France, declared in May, 1806; and the President offered, unasked, a pledge to the French emperor, that this should be insisted upon. Whether he meant to make it easier for Napoleon and harder for Great Britain to respond to the act of May is a question impossible to answer; but the opponents of the policy he was pursuing were careful to point out that the act of May said nothing whatever, either of this or any other blockade; that when, the year before, the agreement was made with Erskine, the President did not pretend that the orders in council included blockades; and that it was remarkable that he should forget his own declaration regarding the monstrous spoliation of a few months before by the French, under the Rambouillet decree, and yet remember this British order of blockade of four years before, which everybody else had forgotten. Indeed, so completely had it passed out of mind, that the

American minister in London, Mr. Pinkney, was obliged to ask the British foreign secretary whether that order had been revoked or was still considered as in force. It had never been formally withdrawn, was the answer, though it had been comprehended in the subsequent order in council of January, 1807. England refused, however, to recall specifically this blockade of 1806, for that would have been construed as a recognition of Napoleon's right to demand an abandonment of her " new principles of blockade ; " but in fact — as the British minister in Washington afterward acknowledged — the recall of the order in council of 1807 would have annulled the order of blockade of 1806, which it had absorbed.

The truth is, the whole negotiation was a trial of skill at diplomatic fence, in which England would not yield an inch to the United States or to France. Madison and his party were more than willing to aid Napoleon; and Napoleon hoped to defeat both his antagonists by turning their swords against each other. A quite different result would have followed had France been as willing as England apparently was that the commercial edicts should be considered without regard to other questions; or if the American Executive had insisted that it would accept their unconditional revocation, pure and simple and not otherwise, from either power, as was contemplated in the act of May, 1810. But instead, when Congress rose in March, 1811, it left behind it an act renewing

non-intercourse with England, in accordance with
Napoleon's demand that the United States should
" cause their rights to be respected by the English." This meant war.

# CHAPTER XIX

In May, 1811, there occurred one of those accidents which happen on purpose, and often serve as a relief when the public temper is in an exasperated and almost dangerous condition. This was the fight between the American frigate President, of forty-four guns, and the English sloop-of-war Little Belt, of eighteen guns. This vessel belonged to the British squadron which was ordered to the American coast to break up the trade from the United States to France; and the President was one of the few ships the government had for the protection of its commerce. The ships met a few miles south of Sandy Hook, chased each other in turn, then fired into each other without any reasonable pretext for the first shot, which each accused the other of having fired. The loss on board the English ship, in an encounter which lasted only a few minutes, was over thirty in killed and wounded, while only a single man was slightly wounded on board the President. It was, as Mr. Madison said, an "occurrence not unlikely to bring on repetitions," and that these would "probably end in an open rupture or a better under-

standing, as the calculations of the British government may prompt or dissuade from war." This
certainly was obvious enough ; though it would be
a great deal easier for England to bring on a war
than to avert it, in the angry mood in which the
majority of the Democratic party then was. But
Mr. Madison preserved his equanimity. Considering his old proclivity for France, and his old dislike
of England, his impartiality between them is rather
remarkable. But his aim was still to keep the
peace while he abated nothing of the well-founded
complaints he had against both powers. When a
new Congress assembled in the autumn he was careful to point out in his message the delinquencies of
France as well as the offenses of England. He
insisted that while England should have acknowledged the Berlin and Milan decrees to be revoked
and have acted accordingly, France showed no disposition to repair the many wrongs she had inflicted
upon American merchants, and had lately imposed
such " rigorous and unexpected restrictions " upon
commerce that it would be necessary, unless they
were speedily discontinued, to meet them by
" corresponding restrictions on importations from
France."

This tone is even more pronounced in his letters for some following months. If anything, it
is France rather than England that seems to be
looked upon as the chief offender, with whom there
was the greater danger of armed collision. A fortnight after Congress had assembled he wrote to

Barlow, the new minister to France, that though justified in assuming the French decrees to be so far withdrawn that a withdrawal of the British orders might be looked for, " yet the manner in which the French government has managed the repeal of the decrees, and evaded a correction of other outrages, has mingled with the conciliatory tendency of the repeal as much of irritation and disgust as possible." " In fact," he adds, " without a systematic change from an appearance of crafty contrivance and insatiate cupidity, for an open, manly, and upright dealing with a nation whose example demands it, it is impossible that good-will can exist; and that the ill-will which her policy aims at directing against her enemy should not, by her folly and iniquity, be drawn off against herself." French depredations upon American commerce in the Baltic were " kindling a fresh flame here," and, if they were not stopped, " hostile collisions will as readily take place with one nation as the other ; " nor would there be any hesitation in sending American frigates to that sea, " with orders to suppress by force the French and Danish depredations," were it not for the " danger of rencounters with British ships of superior force in that quarter."

By this time, however, Congress, under the lead of younger, vigorous men — chief among them Clay and Calhoun — panting for leadership and distinction, was beginning its clamor for war with England. How much respect had Madison for

this movement, and how much faith in it? A
letter to Jefferson of February 7 answers both
questions. Were he not evidently amused, he
would seem to be contemptuous. " To enable the
Executive to step at once into Canada," he says,
" they have provided, after two months' delay,
for a regular force requiring twelve to raise it,
and after three months for a volunteer force, on
terms not likely to raise it at all for that object.
The mixture of good and bad, avowed and disguised motives, accounting for these things, is curious enough, but not to be explained in the compass
of a letter." This is not the tone of either hope
or fear. If war was in his mind at that time, it
was not war with England. Three weeks later he
writes to Barlow at Paris. On various points of
negotiation between that minister and the French
government, he observes much that " suggests distrust rather than expectation." He complains of
delay, of vagueness, of neglect, of discourtesy, of
a disregard of past obligations as to the liberation of ships and cargoes seized, and of late con-
demnations of ships captured in the Baltic ; and
concerning all these and other grievances he says :
" We find so little of explicit dealing or substan-
tial redress mingled with the compliments and
encouragements, which cost nothing because they
mean nothing, that suspicions are unavoidable ; and
if they be erroneous, the fault does not lie with
those who entertain them." He believed that
France, in asking for a new treaty, which he thinks

unnecessary, is only seeking to gain time in order to take advantage of future events. The commercial relations between the two countries are so intolerable that trade "will be prohibited if no essential change take place." Unless there be indemnity for the great wrongs committed under the Rambouillet decree, and for other spoliations, he declares that "there can be neither cordiality nor confidence here; nor any restraint from self-redress in any justifiable mode of effecting it." The letter concludes with the emphatic assertion that, if dispatches soon looked for "do not exhibit the French government in better colors than it has yet assumed, there will be but one sentiment in this country; and I need not say what that will be."

Congress all this while was lashing itself into fury against England. The ambitious young leaders of the Democratic party in the House were, so to speak, "spoiling for a fight," and they chose to have it out with England rather than with France. Not that there was not quite as much reason for resentment against France as against England. Some, indeed, of the more hot-headed were anxious for war with both; but these were of the more impulsive kind, like Henry Clay, who laughed in scorn at the doubt that he could not at a blow subdue the Canadas with a few regiments of Kentucky militia. But war with England was determined upon, partly because the old enmity toward her made that intolerable which to the old affection for France was a burden lightly borne; and partly because the instinctive jealousy of the commercial interest, on the part of the planter-interest, preferred that policy which would do the most harm to the North. On April 1, 1812, just five weeks after the writing of this letter to Barlow, Mr. Madison sent to Congress a message of five lines recommending the immediate passage of an act to impose " a general embargo on all vessels now in port or hereafter arriving for the period of sixty days." It was meant to be a secret measure; but the intention leaked out in two or three places, and the news was hurried North by several of the Federalist members in time to enable some of their constituents to send their ships to sea before the act was passed. Nor, probably, was it a surprise to anybody; for war with England had been the topic of debate in one aspect or another all winter, and the purpose of the party in power was plain to everybody. That the embargo was intended as a preparation for war was frankly acknowledged. An act was speedily passed, though the period was extended from sixty to ninety days. Within less than sixty days, however, another message from the President recommended a declaration of war. On June 3 the Committee on Foreign Relations, of which Calhoun was chairman, reported in favor of " an immediate appeal to arms," and the next day a declaratory act was passed. Of the seventy-nine affirmative votes in the House, forty-eight

were from the South and West, and of the other
thirty-one votes from the Northern States, fourteen
were from Pennsylvania alone.   Of the forty-nine
votes against it, thirty-four were from the Northern
States, including two from Pennsylvania.   On the
17th, a fortnight later, the bill was got through
the Senate by a majority of six.

Mr. Madison for years had opposed a war with
England as unwise and useless, — unwise, because
the United States was not in a condition to go to
war with the greatest naval power in the world;
and useless, because the end to be reached by war
could be gained more certainly, and at infinitely
less cost, by peaceful measures.   The situation had
not changed.   Indeed, up to within a month of
the message recommending an embargo as a precursor of war, his letters show that, if he thought
war was inevitable, it must be with France, not
England.   But the faction determined upon war
must have at their command an administration to
carry out that policy.   Their choice was not limited to Madison for an available candidate.   Who-
ever was nominated by the Democrats was sure
to be chosen, and Madison had two formidable
rivals in James Monroe, secretary of state, and De
Witt Clinton, mayor of New York, both eager for
war.   The choice depended on that question and
between the embargo message of April 1 and the
war message of June 1, the nomination was given
to Madison by the congressional caucus.   It was
understood, and openly asserted at the time by the

opponents of the administration, that the nomination was the price of a change of policy. At the next session of Congress, before a year had passed away, Mr. Quincy said in the House: "The great mistake of all those who reasoned concerning the war and the invasion of Canada, and concluded that it was impossible that either should be seriously intended, resulted from this, that they never took into consideration the connection of both those events with the great election for the chief magistracy which was then pending. It was never sufficiently considered by them that plunging into a war with Great Britain was among the conditions on which the support for the presidency was made dependent." The assertion, so plainly aimed at Madison, passed unchallenged, though the charge of any distinct bargain was vehemently denied.

If Mr. Madison's conscience was not always vigorous enough to enable him to resist temptation, it was so sensitive as to prompt him to look for excuses for yielding. In a sense this was to his credit as one of the better sort of politicians, without assuming it to be akin to that hypocrisy which is the homage vice pays to virtue. Perhaps it was this sentiment which led him to accept so readily the pretended disclosures of John Henry, and to make the use of them he did. These were contained in twenty-four letters, for which the President, apparently without hesitation, paid fifty thousand dollars. On March 9 he sent them to Congress with a message, and on the same day, in

a letter to Jefferson, alludes to them as " this
discovery, or rather formal proof of the coöperation between the Eastern Junto and the British
cabinet." In the message he intimates that this
secret agent was sent directly by the British government to Massachusetts to foment disaffection, to
intrigue " with the disaffected for the purpose of
bringing about resistance to the laws, and eventu-
ally, in concert with a British force, of destroying
the Union " and reannexing the Eastern States to
England. In the war message of June 1 these
charges are repeated as among the reasons for an
appeal to arms. Mr. Calhoun's committee followed
this lead and improved upon it in the report recommending an immediate declaration of war. The
Henry affair was declared an " act of still greater
malignity " than any of the other outrages against
the United States of which Great Britain had been
guilty, and that which " excited the greatest hor-
ror." The incident was seized upon, apparently,
to answer a temporary purpose, and then, so far as
Mr. Madison was concerned, was permitted to sink
into oblivion. In the hundreds of pages of his
published letters, written in later life, in which he
reviews and explains so many of the events of his
public career, there is no allusion whatever to the
Henry disclosures, which in 1812 were held, with
the ruin of American commerce and the impressment of thousands of American citizens, as an
equally just cause for war. In truth there was
nothing whatever in these disclosures, for which

was paid an amount equal to the salary of half a presidential term, to warrant the assumptions of either Mr. Madison's messages or Mr. Calhoun's report. The man had been sent, at his own suggestion, early in 1809, by the governor of Canada to Massachusetts to learn the state of affairs there and observe the drift of public opinion. His national proclivity — he was an Irishman — to conspiracy and revolution had led him to see in the dissatisfaction with the embargo a determination in the New England people to destroy the Union, reannex themselves to England, and return to the flesh-pots of the colonial period. To learn how far gone they were in these designs, to put himself in intimate relations with the leading conspirators and to bring them into communication with Sir James Craig, the governor-general of Canada, that sufficient aid should come through him at the proper moment from the British government, was Henry's mission. Of this truly Irish plot Henry was the villain and Craig the fool; but it is hardly possible that three years afterward Madison and his friends, with all the letters spread before them, could really have been the dupes.

Henry went to Boston and remained there about three months, living at a tavern. He found out nothing because there was nothing to be found out. He knew nobody, and nobody of any note knew him, and all the information he sent to Craig might have been, and doubtless was, picked up in the ordinary political gossip of the tavern bar-

room, or culled from the columns of the newspapers of both parties. He compromised nobody,
for — as Mr. Monroe, as secretary of state, testi-
fied in a report to the Senate — he named no person or persons in the United States who had,
" in any way or manner whatever, entered into
or countenanced the project or views " of himself
and Craig; and all he had to say was pointless
and unimportant, except so far as his opinions
might have some interest as those of a shrewd
observer of public events. Indeed, his own conclusion was that there was no conspiracy in the
Eastern States; that the Federal party was strong
enough to keep the peace with England; and that
there was no talk of disunion, nor any likelihood of
it unless it should be brought about by war. The
correspondence itself showed, in a letter from
Robert Peel, then secretary to Lord Liverpool,
that the letters of Henry were found, as a matter
of course, among Canadian official papers, as they
related to public affairs; but they had either never
attracted any attention or had been entirely forgotten, and Lord Liverpool was quite ignorant of
any " arrangement or agreement " that had been
made between the governor of Canada and his
emissary to New England. It was only because
of his failure to get any reward from the British
government or from Craig's successor in Canada,
for what he was pleased to call his services, that
the adventurer came to Washington in search of a
market for himself and his papers. He came at

an opportune moment. Notwithstanding the secretary of state frankly declared, that neither by writing nor by word of mouth did the man implicate by name anybody in the United States; notwithstanding one of the letters was evidence, the more conclusive because incidental, that the British secretary of state had known nothing of this mission contrived between Henry and Craig, — yet Mr. Madison pronounced the letters to be the "formal proof of the coöperation between the Eastern Junto and the British cabinet." The charge was monstrous, for this pretended proof had no existence. If the President, however, could persuade himself that the story was true, it would help him to justify himself to himself for a change of policy, the result of which would be the coveted renomination for the presidency.

Not that there had never been talk of disunion in New England. There had been in years past, as there was to be in years to come. But talk of that kind did not belong exclusively to that particular period, nor was it confined to that particular region of country. Ever since the adoption of the Constitution the one thing that orators, North and South, inside the halls of Congress and outside them, were agreed upon was, that in all debate there was one argument, equally good on both sides, to which there could be no reply; that in all legislation there was one possible supreme move that would bring all the wheels of government to a dead stop. The solemn warning or the angry

threat was always in readiness for instant use,
that the bonds of the Union, in one or another
contingency, were to be rent asunder. But so
frequent had been these warning cries of the coming wolf that they were listened to with indifference, except when some positive act indicated real
danger, as in the Jefferson-Madison " resolutions
of '98." It was easy, therefore, to alarm the public with confessions of a secret emissary, as he pretended, who had turned traitor to the government
which had employed him and to the conspirators
to whom he had been sent; and the more repre-
hensible was it, therefore, in a President of the
United States, to make the use that was made of
this story, which an impartial examination would
have shown was essentially absurd and infamously
false. Mr. Madison's intelligence is not to be
impugned. He was too sagacious, as well as too
unimpassioned a man, to be taken in by the ingenious tale of such an adventurer as Henry. In a
letter to Colonel David Humphreys, written the
next spring, in defense of the policy of commercial restrictions, he says : " I have never allowed
myself to believe that the Union was in danger, or
that a dissolution of it could be desired, unless by
a few individuals, if such there be, in desperate
situations or of unbridled passions." New England, he continues, " would be the greatest loser
by such an event, and not likely therefore deliberately to rush into it." " On what basis," he
asks, " could New England and Old England form

commercial stipulations?" Their commercial jealousy, he contends, forbade an alliance between them, for that was "the real source of our Revolution." He closes with the significant assertion that, "if there be links of common interest between the two countries, they would connect the Southern and not the Northern States with that part of Europe." How, then, could he seriously accept Henry's pretended disclosures as "formal proof," as he wrote to Jefferson at that time, "of the coöperation between the Eastern Junto and the British cabinet"? By the Eastern Junto is meant the Federal party, or at least the influential and able leaders of that party; and he could not consider, nor would he have spoken of them as "a few individuals, if such there be, in desperate situations or of unbridled passions." He accepted, then, the Henry story in spite of his deliberate opinions, as a help to involve the country in a party war.

Even at the risk of some prolixity it is needful to follow the course of events that led to this war a little farther; for here was the culmination of Mr. Madison's career, and from his course in shaping and directing these events we best learn what manner of man he was, and where his true place is among the public men of our earlier history. For a year and a half the United States had acted on the assumption that France had recalled her decrees, and that England had not revoked her orders. The extracts from Mr. Madison's letters, given on previous pages, show his conviction that the revo-

cation of either decrees or orders was practically
no more true of one power than it was of the other.
The government of the United States, nevertheless,
submitted to the one, and against the other it first
reënacted the non-intercourse act, then proclaimed
an embargo preparatory to war, and finally declared
war. Yet the whole world knew, and nobody so
surely as the emperor of France, that the Berlin
and Milan decrees had never been formally repealed
at all ; meanwhile French outrages upon American
commerce had continued, and all redress so per-
sistently refused that, so late as the last week in
February, 1812, the President intimated that war
— war with France, not England — might prove
the only remedy. But he suddenly yielded to the
clamors of the war party at home, whatever may
have been his motive. Then, and not till then,
were the decrees actually revoked by Napoleon.
In May, 1812, more than a month after the President had recommended an embargo, the hostile
purport of which was so well understood, a decree
was proclaimed by the emperor which for the first
time really revoked those of Berlin and Milan.
True, it was dated — " purported to be dated," it
was said in an official English document — April,
1811. But that was of no moment ; the essential
point was, that it had never seen the light ; that
any hint of its existence had never been given to
the American government, or its representatives
abroad, till the United States had taken measures
to " cause their rights to be respected by the Eng-

lish," which was the original condition of a revocation of the decrees. Its ostensible date was when the news reached France that non-intercourse had been again enforced against England in March, 1811; but its promulgation was to all intents and purposes the real date, when news reached France, in April or May, 1812, that war against England was finally determined upon.

The Duke of Bassano, the French minister, had not, moreover, brought out this year-old decree without pressure from the American minister, Barlow. The President had written Barlow, in that February letter already quoted, that if his expected dispatches did not " exhibit the conduct of the French government in better colors than it has yet assumed, there will be but one sentiment in this country, and I need not say what that will be." When the dispatches came, Mr. Madison received no assurances of redress for past wrongs and no promises for the future ; but he learned, on the contrary, that Bassano, in a recent report to the emperor, had referred to the decrees of Berlin and Milan as still in force against all neutral nations which submitted to the seizure of their ships by the British when containing contraband goods or enemy's property. Naturally the British ministry was not slow in presenting this precious acknowledgment to the United States as a proof that she had all along been in the wrong, and that in common justice to England the non-importation act should now be repealed. The assurance was at the

same time repeated, possibly in a tone of considerable satisfaction, that when Napoleon really should
revoke his decrees Great Britain was ready, as she
always had been, to follow his example with her
orders.   It was an awkward dilemma for the President and his minister to France.   But by this
time, the Presidential nomination impending, Mr.
Madison had made up his mind what to do.   He
was not exactly a wolf; neither was Great Britain
a lamb; but the argument he used was the argument of the fable.   Instead of advising — Bassano
having declared the decrees still in force — a
repeal of the non-importation act, as Great Britain
claimed was in justice and comity her due, he recommended a war measure.   But Barlow evidently
felt himself to be under some decent restraint of
logic and consistency.   He urged upon the French
minister the necessity now of a positive and impe-
rial declaration that the decrees, so far as regarded
the United States, were absolutely revoked ; for
this recent assertion of Bassano, that they were still
in force, put the United States in an attitude both
towards France and England utterly and absurdly
in the wrong.   Barlow represented that, should the
revocation be extended only to the United States,
Great Britain would not for that alone repeal her
orders.   In that case France would lose nothing
of the advantage of her present position, while
everything would be lost should the United States
be compelled to repeal her non-importation laws
against England.   Bassano was quick to see the

necessity of jumping into the bramble-bush and scratching his eyes in again, and he then produced his year-old edict. Being a year old, it of course covered all questions. But was it a year old? Who knew? It had never been published? No, the duke said; but it had been shown to Mr. Jonathan Russell, who at that time was chargé d'affaires at Paris. Mr. Russell denied it, though a denial was hardly needed. He would not have ventured to withhold information so important from his government; and it was evident, from the tone of his dispatches of a subsequent date, that he had no suspicion of its existence. For he had maintained it, as a point of " national honor," that the revocation of the French decrees must have preceded the President's proclamation of November 1, 1810; and this he would not have dared to do had he known that the actual revocation by the French minister was not made till six months after the date of the President's proclamation, and was then made secretly.

However, as if to defeat all these machinations of France and the United States, Great Britain immediately recalled her orders in council, when, in May, 1812, the Duke of Bassano announced the edict of April, 1811, revoking the Berlin and Milan decrees, though so far only as they concerned American vessels. The declaration of war of June 18 had not reached England, and there was still a chance for peace. Foster, the late English minister to the United States, learned at Halifax — where he had stopped on his way home — that

the orders in council were repealed, and he took
immediate steps to bring about an armistice between the naval commanders on the coast of Nova
Scotia, and between the governor of Canada and
the American general, Dearborn, in command of
the frontier. The government at Washington, however, refused to ratify any suspension of hostilities.
Some negotiations followed, but, decrees and orders
being out of the way, there was nothing left to
negotiate about except the question of impressment.
Upon that question the two governments were as
wide apart as ever, and not in the least likely to
come together.    Mr. Madison determined that on
that ground alone the war should go on.    It had
been as good and sufficient ground for such a war
any time for the past dozen years ; but whether it
could be settled by an appeal to arms was a question of possibilities and probabilities by which both
Jefferson and Madison had hitherto been ruled.
Was that still the essential question ?   With the
result came the answer.    Two years later the administration was glad to accept a treaty of peace
in which impressment was not even alluded to.
Great Britain did not relinquish by a syllable her
assumed right to board American ships in search of
British seamen ; and the administration instructed
its peace commissioners not even to ask that she
should.

# CHAPTER XX

## CONCLUSION

EARLY in the war Mr. Madison said to a friend, in a letter " altogether *private* and written in confidence," that the way to make the conflict both " short and successful would be to convince the enemy that he was to contend with the whole and not part of the nation." That it was a war of a party, and not of the people, was a discouragement to himself, however the enemy may have regarded it, which he could never see any way of overcoming. He could not listen to an opponent nor learn anything from disaster. " If the war must continue," said Webster within a year of its end, " go to the ocean. Let it no longer be said that not one ship of force, built by your hands since the war, yet floats. If you are seriously contending for maritime rights, go to the theatre where those rights can be defended. . . . There the united wishes and exertions of the nation will go with you. Even our party divisions, acrimonious as they are, cease at the water's edge. . . . In protecting naval interests by naval means, you will arm yourself with the whole power of national sentiment, and may command the whole abundance of national forces." Taking now in one view the events of those years, it is easy to see in our generation how mad were Madison and his party to turn deaf ears to such considerations as these. Their force and wisdom had already been proved by eighteen months of disaster on land, which had made the war daily more and more unpopular ; and by brilliant success for a time at sea, when each fresh victory was hailed with universal enthusiasm. " Our little naval triumphs," was the President's way of speaking of the latter ; and the only importance he seems to have seen in them was, that they excited some " rage and jealousy " in England and moved her to increase her naval force. How could Mr. Madison expect that the whole and not a part only of the nation could uphold an administration which, after eighteen months of fighting, could be reproached on the floor of Congress with not having launched a ship since the war was begun ? Or did he only choose to remember that the navy, which alone so far had brought either success or honor to the national arms, was the creation of the Federalists in spite of the Jeffersonian policy ? It surely would have been wiser to try to propitiate New England, with which he was in perpetual worry and conflict, by enlisting it in a naval war in which it had some faith. A large proportion of her people would have been glad to escape idleness and poverty at home for service at sea, though they were reluctant to aid in a vain attempt to conquer Canada.

*Battle of Lake Erie*

Even to that purpose, however, Massachusetts
contributed, in the second campaign of 1814, more
recruits than any other single State; and New England more than all the Southern States together.
New England could have given no stronger proof
of her loyalty, if only Mr. Madison had known
how to turn it to advantage. He was absolutely
deaf and blind to it; but his ears were quick to
hear and his eyes to see, when he learned presently that the New Englanders were seriously cal-
culating the value of the Union under such rule
as they had had of late. It was not often that he
relieved himself by intemperate language, but he
could not help saying now, in writing to Governor
Nicholas of Virginia, that "the greater part of the
people in that quarter have been brought by their
leaders, aided by their priests, under a delusion
scarcely exceeded by that recorded in the period
of witchcraft; and the leaders themselves are becoming daily more desperate in the use they make
of it." The "delusion" was taking a practical
direction. Mr. Madison had learned before the
letter was written that a convention was about to
meet at Hartford, the object of which was to weigh
in a balance, upon the one side, the continuation of
such government as that of the last two or three
years, and, upon the other side, the value of the
Union. He ardently hoped that the commissioners, then assembled at Ghent, would agree upon a
treaty; and there seemed to be no good reason
why there should not be peace when nothing was

to be said of the cause of the war, no apology
demanded for the past, and no stipulation for the
future.  But if by any chance the commissioners
should fail, Mr. Madison saw in the Hartford Convention the huge shadow of a coming conflict more
difficult to deal with than a foreign war.  It was
the first step in dead earnest for the formation of
a Northern Confederacy, and it is quite possible
he may have felt that he was not the man for such
a crisis.  Every line of the letter pulsates with
anxiety.  The only consoling thought in it is that
without " foreign coöperation revolt and separa-
tion will hardly be risked," and to such coöperation he hoped a majority of the New England
people would not consent.  A treaty of peace, however, came to save him and the Union.  Within
a few weeks the administration papers were laugh-
ing at Harrison Gray Otis of Boston, who had
started for Washington as the representative of
the Hartford Convention, but turned back at the
news of peace ; and were advertising him as
missing under the name of Titus Oates.  It was,
however, the hysterical laugh of recovery from a
terrible fright.

If ambition to be a second time President led
Mr. Madison to consent against his own better
judgment to a war with England, he paid a heavy
penalty.  It was the act of a party politician and
not of a statesman ; for the country was no more
prepared for a war in 1812, when as a politician
he assented to it, than it had been for the previous

half dozen years when as a statesman he had
opposed it. He gave the influence of the United
States in support of a despotism that aimed at
the subjugation of all Europe; he threw a fresh
obstacle in the way of that power to which Europe
could chiefly look to resist a common enemy; and
he did both under the pretense that the just complaints of the United States were greater against
one of these powers than against the other. He
declared war mainly to redress a wrong which
ceased to exist before a blow was struck; he then
rejected an offer of peace because another wrong
was still persisted in; but finally, of his own motion, he accepted a treaty in which the assumed
cause of war was not even alluded to.

That Mr. Madison was not a good war President, either by training or by temperament, was,
if it may be said of any man, his misfortune rather
than his fault. But it was his fault rather than
his misfortune that he permitted himself to be
dragged in a day into a line of conduct which the
sober judgment of years had disapproved. He
is usually and most justly regarded as a man of
great amiability of character; of unquestionable
integrity in all the purely personal relations of
life; of more than ordinary intellectual ability
of a solid, though not brilliant, quality; and a
diligent student of the science of government, the
practice of which he made a profession. But he
was better fitted by nature for a legislator than
for executive office, and his fame would have been

more spotless, though his position would have been less exalted, had his life been exclusively devoted to that branch of government for which he was best fitted. It was not merely that for the sake of the Presidency he plunged the country into an unnecessary war ; but when it was on his hands he neither knew what to do with it himself nor how to choose the right men who did know.

It is our amiable weakness — if one may venture to say so of the American people — that all our geese are swans, or rather eagles ; that we are apt to mistake notoriety for reputation ; that it is the popular belief of the larger number that he who, no matter how, has reached a distinguished position, is by virtue of that fact a great and good man. This is not less true, in a measure, of Mr. Madison than of some other men who have been Presidents, and of still more who have thought that they deserved to be. But, if that false estimate surrounds his name, there is a strong undercurrent of opinion, common among those whose business or whose pleasure it is to look beneath the surface of things historical, that he was wanting in strength of character and in courage. He did not lack discernment as to what was wisest and best ; but he was too easily influenced by others, or led by the hope of gaining some glittering prize which ambition coveted, to turn his back upon his own convictions. It was this weakness which swept him beyond his depth into troubled waters where his struggles were hopeless. Had he refused

to assume the responsibility of a war which his
judgment condemned, and which he should have
known that he wanted the peculiar ability to bring
to a successful and honorable conclusion, he might
never have been President, but his fame would
have been of a higher order. History might
have overlooked the act of political fickleness in
his earlier career, which was so warmly resented
by many of his contemporaries. Abandonment
of party is too common and often too justifiable
to be accounted as necessarily a crime; and it
can rarely be said with positiveness, whatever the
probabilities, that a political deserter is certainly
moved by base motives. It is rather from *ex post
facto* than from immediate evidence, as in Madison's case, that a just verdict is likely to be
reached. But there can be neither doubt nor mistake as to the President's management of foreign
affairs during the two years preceding the declaration of war against England; nor of the remarkable incompetence which he showed in rallying the
moral and material forces of the nation to meet an
emergency of his own creation.

Opposition to war generally and therefore opposition to an army and navy were sound cardinal
principles in the Jeffersonian school of politics.
Mr. Madison was curiously blind to the logical
consequences of this doctrine; he could not see,
or he would not consider, that, when war seemed
advisable to an administration, the result must
depend mainly upon the success of the appeal to

the people for their countenance and help.  But he
unwisely sought to raise and employ an army for
the invasion and conquest of the territory of the
enemy in spite of the opposition of a large proportion of the wealthiest and most intelligent people
in the country ; while at the same time he refused
to see any promise or any presage in a naval warfare which had opened with unexpected brilliancy,
and would, had it been followed up, have been
sure of popular support.  His title to fame rests,
with the multitude, upon the fact that he was one
of the earlier Presidents of the republic.  But it
is that period of his career which least entitles him
to be remembered with gratitude and respect by
his countrymen.

Its crowning humiliation came with the capture
of Washington in August, 1814, when the British
admiral, Cockburn, entered the Hall of Representatives, at the head of a band of followers, and
springing into the speaker's chair shouted : " Shall
this harbor of Yankee Democracy be burned ?
All for it will say, Aye ! "   Early in the war
Madison had written to Jefferson, " We do not
apprehend invasion by land," — the one thing, it
would seem, that a commander-in-chief should
have apprehended, whose single aim was the invasion and conquest of the enemy's territory.
His devotion to this one purpose, to the exclusion of any other idea of either offense or defense,
and in spite of continued failure, was almost an
infatuation.  Within a year of that expression of

confidence to Mr. Jefferson the whole coast was blockaded from the eastern end of Long Island Sound to the mouth of the Mississippi. For a year before Washington was taken, the shores of Chesapeake Bay were harassed and raided and devastated by a blockading force, till the people were reduced almost to the condition of a conquered country. Two months before the British commanders, Ross and Cockburn, went up the Potomac, Mr. Gallatin, who was then in London, had informed the President that the fleet was to be reinforced for that very purpose; but neither he nor Congress took any effective measures to meet a danger so imminent. Their eyes were fixed with a far-off gaze across the Northern border, while only five hundred regular troops, a body of untrained militia who had never heard the whistle of a bullet, and a few gunboats on the Potomac, guarded the national capital against a British fleet, a thousand marines, and thirty-five hundred men from Wellington's best regiments. The President fleeing in one direction with the secretary of war, the secretary of state, and the general in command; Mrs. Madison fleeing in another, with her reticule filled with silver spoons snatched up in haste as she left the White House; [1] behind them all as they fled, the horizon

[1] Paul Jennings, who was a slave and the body servant of Mr. Madison, says in his *Reminiscences:* "It has often been stated in print, that when Mrs. Madison escaped from the White House, she cut out from the frame the large portrait of Washington (now in one of the parlors there) and carried it off. This is totally false.

red with the blaze of the largest navy yard in the
country and of all the public buildings, but one, of
the capital, — these incidents are an amazing com-
mentary on the early assertion that invasion was
not to be apprehended.

The end of this wretched war, which has been
foolishly called the second war of independence,
came four months afterward. Never was a peace
so welcome as this was on all sides. England was
exhausted with the long contest with Napoleon;
and now, that being over, as there was no practical
question to differ about with the United States,
the ministry were not unwilling to listen to the
demands of the commercial and manufacturing
classes. In America so great was the universal
joy that the Federalists and the Democrats forgot their differences and their hates, and wept
and laughed by turns in each other's arms and
kissed each other like women. One party was delivered from calamities for which, if continued

She had no time for doing it. It would have required a ladder to
get it down. All she carried off was the silver in her reticule, as
the British were thought to be but a few squares off, and were
expected every moment. John Suse (a Frenchman, then door-
keeper, and still [1865] living), and Magraw, the President's
gardener, took it down and sent it off on a wagon, with some
large silver urns and such other valuables as could hastily be got
hold of. When the British did arrive, they ate up the very
dinner, and drank the wines, etc., that I had prepared for the
President's party." On a previous page he had related that:
"Mrs. Madison ordered dinner to be ready at three as usual; I
set the table myself, and brought up the ale, cider, and wine, and
placed them in the coolers, as all the cabinet and several military
gentlemen and strangers were expected."

much longer, there seemed only one desperate and dreaded remedy ; the other was overjoyed to back out of a blunder which was the straight and broad road to national ruin. Of all men, Mr. Madison had the most reason to be glad for a safe deliverance from the consequences of his own want of foresight and want of firmness. Less than two years remained to him of his public career. In that brief period much was forgotten and more forgiven — as our national way is — in the promise of a great prosperity to be speedily achieved in the released energies of a vigorous and industrious people. He had not again to choose between differing factions of his own party, nor to carry out a policy against the will of a formidable opposition. To the Federalists hardly a name was left in the progress of events at home and abroad; while all immediate vital questions of difference vanished, the party in power remained in almost undisputed ascendency. The most important Democratic measures it then insisted upon were a national bank and a protective tariff. To the establishment of a bank Mr. Madison assented against his own conviction that any provision could be found for it in the Constitution ; and a tariff, both for revenue and for the protection and encouragement of American industry, he agreed with his party was the true policy.

For nearly twenty years after his retirement to Montpellier — a name which, with rare exceptions, he always spelled correctly, and not in the American way — it was his privilege to live a watchful observer of the prosperity of his country. If it ever occurred to him in his secret soul that at the period of his preëminence he had done anything to arrest that prosperity, he gave no sign. He loved rather to remember and sometimes to recall to others the part he had taken in the nurture of the young republic in the feeble days of its infancy. Of his own administration and the events of that time he had much less to say than of the true interpretation of the Constitution, of the intent of its framers, and the circumstances that influenced their deliberations. His voluminous correspondence shows the bent of his mind as a legislator and a student of fundamental law ; and on that, rather than on his ability and success as the chief magistrate of the nation, rests his true fame.

These twenty years, though passed in retirement, were not years of leisure. " I have rarely," he wrote in 1827, " during the period of my public life, found my time less at my disposal than since I took my leave of it ; nor have I the consolation of finding, that as my powers of application necessarily decline, the demands on them proportionally decrease." Much as he wrote upon questions of an earlier period, there were no topics of the current time that did not arouse his interest. Upon the subject of slavery he thought much and wrote much and always earnestly and humanely. How to get rid of it was a problem which he never solved to his own satisfaction. Though it was one

he always longed to see through, it never occurred
to him that the way to abolish slavery was — to
abolish it.   How kind he was as a master, Paul
Jennings bears witness.   " I never," he says, " saw
him in a passion, and never knew him to strike
a slave, though he had over a hundred; neither
would he allow an overseer to do it."   He rebuked those who were in fault; but, adds Jennings, he would " never mortify them by doing it
before others."   It will be remembered that on the
first occasion of his being a candidate for public
office he refused to follow the universal Virginian
habit of " treating " the electors.   To the principle
which governed him then he adhered through life,
and his letters show the warm interest he always
took in every phase of the temperance movement.
" I don't think he drank a quart of brandy in
his whole life," says Jennings.   A single glass of
wine was all he ever took at dinner, and this he
diluted with water, when, says the same witness,
" he had hard drinkers at his table who had put
away his choice madeira pretty freely."   This
will go for something, considering the times, with
even the most zealous of the modern supporters
of that cause ; but they must be quite satisfied
to know that " for the last fifteen years of his life
he drank no wine at all."   Consideration for his
own health, always feeble, may have led him to
this abstinence ; but it is rather remarkable that a
man of his position should have held, fifty years
ago, the advanced notions which he certainly did

upon this question, and that the doubt only of
the possibility of enforcing laws for prohibiting
the manufacture and sale of spirits seems to have
withheld him from proposing them.

Social as well as moral questions he discussed
with evident interest and without passion or prejudice. Aside from the party meaning of the term,
he belonged to that school of democracy, now
extinct, which believed that the highest object of
human exertion is to improve man's condition, and
to secure to each the rights which belong to all.
He did not agree with Robert Owen as to meth-
ods; but neither did he reject his schemes as inev-
itably absurd because they were new and untried.
One would not gather from his correspondence
with Frances Wright that this was the notorious
Fanny Wright whom the world chose to consider,
as its way is, a disreputable and probably wicked
woman, inasmuch as she proposed some radical
changes in its social relations which she thought
would be a gain. He gave much attention to
popular education, and all the influence he could
command was devoted, through all the later years
of his life, to the establishment and well-being of
the University of Virginia. Education, he maintained, was the true foundation of civil liberty, and
on it, therefore, rested the welfare and stability of
the republic. It is probable that he would have
drawn a line at difference of color then, simply
because of the difference of condition implied by
color. But he made no such distinction in sex.

Sixty-three years ago he saw his way quite clearly on a question which is a sore trial now to many timid souls. The capacity of "the female mind" for the highest education cannot, he said, "be doubted, having been sufficiently illustrated by its works of genius, of erudition, and of science." The capacity, he assumed, carried with it the right. In short, he was ready always to consider fairly questions relating to the well-being of society which since his time have deeply agitated the country; and he approached them all much in the spirit of the reformer who hopes to leave the world a little better and happier because he has lived in it.

"Mr. Madison, I think," says Paul Jennings, "was one of the best men that ever lived." This is the testimony of an intelligent man whose opportunities of knowing the personal qualities of him of whom he was speaking were more intimate than those of any other person could be except Mrs. Madison. "He was guilty," says Hildreth, "of the greatest political wrong and crime which it is possible for the head of a nation to commit." One saw the private gentleman, always conscientious and considerate in his personal relations to other men; the other judged the public man, moved by ambition, entangled in party ties and supposed party obligations, his moral sense blinded by the necessities of political compromises to reach party ends. It is not impossible to strike a just balance between these opposing estimates, though one is that of a servant, the other that of a learned and judicious historian.

Mr. Madison left a legacy of "Advice to My Country," to be read after his death and to " be considered as issuing from the tomb, where truth alone can be respected, and the happiness of man alone consulted." It is the lesson of his life, as he wished his countrymen to understand it. " The advice," he said, " nearest to my heart and deepest in my convictions is, that the Union of the States be cherished and perpetuated. Let the open enemy to it be regarded as a Pandora with her box opened, and the disguised one as the serpent creeping with his deadly wiles into Paradise." The thoughtful reader, as he turns to the first page of this volume to recall the date of Mr. Madison's death, will hardly fail to note how few the years were before these open and disguised enemies, against whom he warned his countrymen, were found only in that party which he had done so much, from the time of the adoption of the Constitution, to keep in power.

# INDEX

# INDEX